ann finnemore

taking your road trip to happiness

Ann Finnemore

Life in the driving seat © Ann Finnemore

First published in 2016

A CIP catalogue record of this book is available from the British Library.

Published by Goldcrest Books International Ltd
www.goldcrestbooks.com
publish@goldcrestbooks.com

ISBN: 978-1-911505-11-2 (paperback)
ISBN: 978-1-911505-12-9 (.mobi)
ISBN: 978-1-911505-13-6 (.epub)

"This book is a 'must read' for those wishing to change their direction in life. A superb, in depth, but simple guide to self-maintenance. I personally highly recommend this superb offering from Ann Finnemore"

Dan Elliott, Practitioner of Clinical Hypnosis,
Queensland, Australia

"While most other self-help books leave you stuck in first gear, Ann's book offers a truly interactive and practical way to implement life and business change. Straight to the point, with an easy flowing style, I found this more enlightening than a panorama sunroof. Highly recommended."

C Cooper-Hayes, business owner

"Ann writes in a way that a layperson can understand and she is obviously knowledgeable about her subject. The easy way that she writes clearly explains processes to help her readers work out for themselves how best to improve their work and life balance. Really made me think and I found very useful."

D Heron, business owner

DEDICATION

This book is dedicated to all of the people who have supported me on my own journey to become a coach, therapist, business owner and author.

The tutors who taught me the skills; my clients, who teach me new things about the many different ways in which success can be defined and attained; and most of all to my husband, Steve, for his continuing patience, support and good humour throughout the whole process, while succeeding in his own journey.

Without each of these people, my journey would not have been as enjoyable as it has been so far.

TABLE OF CONTENTS

INTRODUCTION

Welcome to the trip of a lifetime

Do you have dreams or hopes that you've had for many years, but you never seem to get close to achieving them? Do you find that no matter how much you want something, you always seem to get derailed on the way to success? Then Life in the Driving Seat has been written for you. This book will enable you to:

- Take control of your life.

- Create your vision of your perfect future.

- Identify the goals and milestones that pave the way to that future.

- Create a plan for success.

- Enjoy the journey to the future you want.

Life in the Driving Seat: taking a road trip to happiness provides a unique approach to enabling you to finally achieve the success you want - on your own terms. Using the analogy of a road trip, you will learn how to take control of your journey to a successful future, planning to take the best route for you and how to cope easily with setbacks along the way. With this book as your companion, you will look forward to your destination whilst also enjoying the experience of travelling itself.

Throughout my life, I have come across many people who have been intending to get to a particular place in their life for years and yet never seem to get any closer to that destination. I was the same myself for many years. Eventually, I found that I'd climbed up pretty high on the career ladder and I discovered that it was assumed that I wanted to carry on climbing until I reached the very top. However, all around me I saw others climbing similar ladders and most of them were working very long hours and suffering from the physical, psychological and emotional effects of stress. This problem came very close to home when my husband, Steve, started to experience the effects of both acute and chronic stress after his workload and responsibilities had increased to ridiculous levels. It got even closer when I noticed that my own well-being and performance were decreasing too. I began to think differently about my life and about what I wanted in my future.

Recalling my jobs over the years, I realised that the roles that I had found most rewarding where those in which I had supported, coached and mentored others. I had done this in education, in the voluntary sector and in corporate teams. Whenever I had been in a role where coaching and mentoring had been an integral part of my work, I had thoroughly enjoyed the experience and had received excellent feedback. Therefore, I decided to build on all of this experience and to start training in life coaching and behavioural change techniques, to enable others to develop the skills and the confidence to discover their own ability to create and to live the life they want.

I also started researching into stress management techniques and the various ways that successful and happy people manage significant changes to their lifestyles. It was through this research that I discovered how changes in mind-set and thinking style can transform a person's ability to achieve what they want. I realised that, due to some positive influences as

I was growing up, I already did some of those things, which explained why I was a little more resilient to stress and more open to change than some of the people around me. I also discovered there was much more that I could do. I decided then to begin to think, dream and plan my future more – to really decide what I wanted to do, how I wanted to live so that I could move into the future that I wanted.

Through my training and experience I have learned that each person has to achieve their goals in the best way possible for them. Each journey to a happy future is a personal one. I have also learned that it helps to have more than just the right mental attitude – success is much more likely if that positive attitude is underpinned with a few practical planning skills too. After all, if you are going to achieve an ambitious, long-term goal, it really helps to know that your plan to achieve it is sound. I realised that this was something I could add to the coaching experience for my clients. Throughout my working life, I've been involved in designing and implementing plans - working on everything from small local projects to major national programmes. I now integrate those skills into coaching to ensure that success becomes inevitable.

I now work with clients to enable them to achieve their dreams and ambitions by developing a healthy and positive mind-set and through learning the skills to plan their journey to success effectively. This way, not only do they reach their destination – they do so with enough energy, motivation and focus to enjoy their new situation and to plan further adventures.

I have used this combined approach throughout *Life in the Driving Seat: taking a road trip to happiness* to bring you a truly practical guide to planning and achieving your dreams. Throughout the book there are activities for you to do which will help you to understand yourself and your journey more deeply and which will ensure you're taking the best route for you to get to the place you want to go to in life.

At the end of each chapter, there is a summary of the chapter's contents *(A glance in the rear view mirror)*. This is to provide you with a helpful reminder of what you have learned from that chapter, and reinforce its key messages.

Are you ready?

To increase your chances of success further, it's worth being aware of the basic characteristics of those people who are successful. Such people:

- have decided that now is the right time. That is to say, they are not just considering making a change in the future, they're actually ready to begin now – it is a decision, not just an idea.

- accept that real change takes time and involves planning. They understand that worthwhile changes often need to be gradual and always need to be sustainable – and that rapid results are very often only short-term ones.

- understand that to achieve what they want they will definitely need to involve others too: for support, to provide expert advice or to teach them new skills.

- are willing to invest in their future – to invest time, money, effort, as needed.

- know that success doesn't mean perfection from day one –there will be slip ups and setbacks. Most importantly, they know that such events are not failures, but are just lessons on the way to achieving their goal.

How to use this book

This book presents a step-by-step guide to making your own personal journey to success and happiness. There are two ways you can use this book:

- Use it as a workbook to start your journey immediately. Reading each chapter and completing the activities in each, before moving on to the next.

or

- Read the book all the way through without doing the activities at first to get a feel for the whole process. Then start at the beginning when you are ready to begin your journey, carrying out each activity as you go.

Whichever method you decide upon, do take time to do each activity as this is a journey of self-discovery as much as it is the journey to your goals, and each activity will increase your chances of a smooth journey to the life you want.

Whenever you see this sign: grab your notebook and pen, or download any related template from the website at www. gettingyouthere.co.uk/life-in-the-driving-seat/resources, as you'll need these for the activity.

At times, you might re-visit an activity or review a particular stage and that's OK. After all, this is a journey of a lifetime, so do what you need to do in order to make this a truly awesome one!

PART ONE
PREPARING FOR THE TRIP OF A LIFETIME

"To travel is to take a journey into yourself"
Danny Kaye

Chapter 1: Getting behind the wheel

To start your journey to get to the future that you really want, the first thing you need to do is to take control of the direction of your life – to get in the driving seat. This is essential, because if you allow someone else to set your destination, dictate the route and make key decisions about the direction and style of driving, you will never get to the place you want to be. **To achieve the life you want, first you must be ready to get into the driver's seat.**

This chapter will enable you to do just that. From the very beginning, you will begin to challenge, and then change, the way you think, feel and behave in relation to your life. You will learn how to stop handing over the controls of your life to others, and start instead to assert yourself as the one behind your life's steering wheel.

Also in this chapter, you will take a look at exactly where you are starting your journey from. For any journey to be successful, it is just as important to recognise and accept the starting point as it is to know the destination. For some of you, the desire to be starting from somewhere other than where you are at this moment might be exactly what's holding you back from starting your personal journey. This chapter will enable you to get over that obstacle and to learn to accept your starting point. As a result, you will be ready to start your journey from your own here and now. After all, where else can you start from?

Accepting the car keys

The first step in the journey to the life they want can be emotionally challenging for some people. The reason some find it challenging to do is because it tackles something that is at the root of why many people fail to achieve the happiness and success they dream of – those beliefs about ourselves and our lives which have underpinned all our actions and decisions up to this point. However, it is important that you do this activity at the very beginning because it lays the firm foundations for your future happiness and success. So don't worry if at first this is an emotional process – the benefits and outcomes will be exciting and fulfilling!

The first activity in this book involves asking yourself a very important question, one which is key to getting the best mind-set for success. Considering this question will begin the process of enabling you to accept the level of responsibility and control that you have over your life. Studies have shown that those who hold themselves responsible for their lives are consistently happier and more successful than those who believe that external factors such as governments, the economy or other people control their circumstances. This recognition of personal responsibility is the biggest factor in success and happiness.

If you believe that your success or failure is solely due to external factors, then your mind will never find ways of succeeding in bringing about the life you want. After all, if you have no control over your situation, then what *could* you do? As a result, your mind will not see opportunities or come up with creative solutions because you've already told yourself that your dreams are impossible. You will stall before you even get going on your journey.

When you live your life this way, you are like a child in the back of the car. You have no say in the way the car is being driven, the route being taken or even the final destination. When you complain that you're not enjoying the journey, or that you don't want to go to where you're being taken, no-one listens. Even when the journey seems pleasant, you are largely unaware of where you are going or whether you'll like where you get to at the journey's end.

What if, instead, you consider the idea that where you are now is a reflection of everything you've believed about yourself and the world? How comfortable are you with the idea that where you are now is a direct result of your own decisions, your own choices and your own beliefs?

Activity

This activity will start your journey to the life you want by moving you from being a passenger in your own life to being in the driving seat. So grab your pen and paper and begin…

PART ONE: The first step in this activity is to ask yourself a very important question. As you ask yourself the question, take time to note down all the answers that come into your head. **Note:** You don't need to analyse the answers just yet – just hear them, and write them down. So, with your pen and paper to hand, ask yourself the following question:

"Why am I not living the life that I want?"

Write down every answer that enters your head. Remember, just write down each one without stopping to analyse or reflect on them as you do. You will do that stage next.

PART TWO: Once you have written down all the answers that came to mind, look down your list and highlight any that identify external factors or people as being responsible. For example, you might feel that you were born into the wrong part of society, or that you were encouraged to study the wrong subjects at school. Perhaps you think the economy has prevented you from achieving your dreams? Maybe you believe your situation is all down to luck (good or bad). Do you blame others for any failures or lack of successes in your life - your parents? Your school? The government? Simply highlight any reason you noted down which blames either other people or external events for the position that you're in today.

If you find that you have highlighted any of your reasons in this way, then you have already identified something that is getting in the way of you achieving the life you want.

Now ask yourself that same question again, and this time note down only those answers which are based on the belief that your life is the product of your choices. **Note: this is not about judgement or blame. It is simply a recognition that you have some control over the direction of your life.**

"Why am I not living the life that I want?"

Read through your answers this time and then ask yourself another a slightly different question now. Grab your pen and paper again, take a good look around at your life and how you are currently feeling about it, and then ask yourself:

"Who (or what) am I holding responsible for how I am living my life at the moment, for how I am feeling right now?"

If the answer that pops into your head now is still anything other than "Me", then beware – you are still giving away your power and control over your life. Once you realise that of course, you can then acknowledge and accept your responsibility and regain control.

Some people find the idea of this level of personal responsibility really hard to handle at first. They feel defensive, angry and insulted at the idea that their life is the result of their own actions. After all, it can feel much more comfortable with someone/something else to blame for our lack of success, happiness or achievement. If this is your reaction, that's OK - simply take time to acknowledge that you feel that way and then start to focus on the freedom that this new way of looking at things can offer.

This is not to deny that many people did have a tough start to life. You might have grown up in far from ideal circumstances and did not have an environment, which encouraged confidence and achievement. Some of you might have grown up with parents who neglected you, or you might have been bullied at school. Others might have suffered childhood ill health, which prevented you from doing well academically. Some of you might have had to leave school as soon as possible, curtailing your education, possibly limiting the career options you had as a teenager. As a result of such things, some people's journeys will take longer than others – I am certainly not saying that everyone's journey to their ideal future is simple or straightforward. The good news is that as an adult you can make decisions to change things. You can now decide whether your future will be everything you want it to be rather than simply being a reflection of your past.

The shift in perspective from seeing your life as the result of chance to one in which you see yourself as in control of your life, is a major step forward in the journey to achieving the life you want. As a coach, enabling clients to make this shift in perspective is often the first step I take with them, and it's why I have this activity at the very start of this book. To help with the process of accepting that some of your past decisions and choices did not help you achieve what you wanted to, it can be useful simply to acknowledge that you made those decisions and choices without full awareness of where you wanted to go. Key decisions and choices might have been made when you were young, or before you had the knowledge and skills that you have today. Reassure yourself that you have learned a lot in your life so far and that those experiences have all contributed to bringing you to where you are today – in a position to move forward into the life you want and ready to start that journey now. That's when you can really start moving on with your life.

Even if you haven't previously recognised the level of control you have in your life and have let others steer your journey, you can take back control now – this very minute. How does that feel?

It isn't really surprising that accepting this responsibility for our situation in life can make some people feel a little nervous at first. The good news is that it soon becomes increasingly liberating. It's quite similar to when you first passed your actual driving test and had to take your car on your own for the first time. Of course it's more nerve-wracking at first than getting lifts or taking public transport, but the freedom it gives you soon becomes the greatest reward you could wish for. It doesn't take long for you to never want to go back to being dependent upon the driving and direction of others.

So, don't worry if acknowledging and accepting that you have considerable control over the direction of your life seems a bit scary at first, it will soon become exhilarating. Every second of every day you have choices to make. Whatever you choose will take you in one direction or another. Even if in the past you haven't recognised these choices, let alone taken advantage of them, you can start to do so straightaway – this very second. The very fact that you have picked up this book means you are already beginning to steer your life. So congratulations on making that choice – to get into the driver's seat of your life. You are now taking control of the direction of your life and are ready to set out on the journey of a lifetime – to the future that you've been dreaming about. This the first of many choices you will make over the coming days, weeks, months and years, which will take you to a place of greater opportunity, greater confidence and greater happiness!

Accepting personal responsibility for your life is incredibly optimistic and empowering. After all, if your life is a reflection of your own beliefs and decisions, then by consciously choosing your beliefs and the decisions you make, you can change your whole life. **You can transform the way you experience your life.**

What about luck?

Our sense of personal responsibility also impacts on whether we view ourselves as lucky or unlucky. Have you noticed how some people seem to have good opportunities open to them wherever they go? Do you wonder why the same chances don't come your way and think that those people are just lucky? How would you feel if you learned that luck has little to do with it? That it was a result of a different perspective on life – one that you could develop too?

It is a natural trait that we tend only to see what we are looking for and what we think is relevant to us. If you were to go shopping specifically for a blue jacket, you'd no doubt find quite a few to try on. However, if at the end of the day you were asked how many brown jackets you had seen, you probably wouldn't be able to answer very accurately. Of course, there are likely to have been many brown jackets in the shops, but because you weren't looking for them you just wouldn't really have noticed them. You'd have been too busy looking for the blue ones.

We develop a similar selective attention filter when we get a new car. Maybe before you had that car you hadn't really noticed that make and model around much. Then, once you are driving it, you see them everywhere. It's as if there has suddenly been a mass production of them in your area. Of course, there are no more than before, but your mind is noticing them now because they are now relevant to you in a way in which they weren't beforehand. This is the same process.

The same is true of opportunities. If you're not open to the fact that they exist, if you're not actually looking for them, they will pass by unnoticed. This is especially so if you are actually looking for the threats or negative things in situations instead, as this is what your mind will take notice of and draw to your attention. Those people who are "lucky" are simply those people who see the opportunities in all situations. They look for the good that can come from life, rather than focusing on the bad, and that's what they find.

So, if you want to improve your "luck", set yourself the task of spotting all the good things and opportunities around you. You might be surprised at just how many more opportunities come your way!

Recognising and accepting your starting point

Have you come across the story of a person who is lost and who stops to ask for directions to their destination only to get the reply *"Well, I wouldn't start from here!"*? It's not a particularly useful response is it? It certainly provides no information, which will help you to get you to where you want to be. You need to know the directions from where you actually are, not from elsewhere.

Although this is obvious when we're talking about actual, physical journeys, it's amazing how few people can see that the same is true of their emotional and psychological journeys too – the journey to their goals and ambitions. Very often, people just don't accept where they are in their lives with respect to one goal or another and so start thinking about how they'll get there from another starting point. It can happen with any sort of goal. In fact, along with not recognising that we have a great deal of control over our own lives, this is one of the most common errors of thinking that gets in the way of personal success.

For example, a person might suffer from low self-esteem made worse by their excess body weight. Their goal is to lose weight and feel better about themselves. They could boost their self-esteem by buying some well-fitting and stylish clothes, or by learning a new skill, both of which are known to improve self-esteem. However, instead they put off buying new clothes, going to the gym or even learning a new skill until they've lost some weight and have improved their confidence. This means that they are actually waiting for their end point before they even start their journey! Not surprisingly, they will find themselves stuck where they are instead of moving forward, always held back by the lack of having the self-confidence they dream of.

I've worked with many clients in exactly this position: they constantly buy clothes that will only fit once they've lost weight, rather than clothes that fit now. Consequently, they never seem to have anything to wear despite having a full wardrobe. In this situation, they are not only depriving themselves of nice clothes to wear, which would begin the process of raising self-esteem and increasing self-confidence, they are also confronted with symbols of what they see as their failure every time they open their wardrobe door. Therefore, their poor self-esteem is reinforced and their chance of moving forward is minimal.

If instead, the person simply accepted their current weight as their starting point and started buying clothes which fit nicely and which look good now, they would be far more likely to find that their self-esteem and confidence start to improve immediately. This improved confidence would then encourage them to get back in control of their lifestyle and body weight. In this way, a virtuous cycle is created in which improved self-esteem feeds further success, improving self-esteem further, and so on.

For clarification, it's worth noting here that acceptance in this sense doesn't mean thinking that everything is as it should be and therefore shouldn't be changed. It simply means accepting that the here and now is our starting point and that planning to start from elsewhere isn't going to get us anywhere. It is about accepting the current situation, without judgement or regret and starting to take our first steps forward.

So, just like any journey, you will achieve your goals only by starting from where you are now. This is true for all of your goals, whatever they are and whatever your current situation is.

Activity

The aim of this activity is to determine your starting point for each aspect of your life or project. This will also help you work out how much progress you want or need to make in each aspect, and provides a way to measure your progress as you go along. The activity is called a Wheel of Life, though you can also have a Wheel of Business too, if your journey is a business project. This exercise is a great first step towards your new future as it enables you to focus your energy on the areas most lacking in your life.

The first step is to decide on the segments that make up your wheel. On the next page are two examples (both are available as A4 downloads from www.gettingyouthere.co.uk/life-in-the-driving-seat/resources); the first is for those wanting to make changes in their life overall, and the second is for those of you planning a business venture. If your destination involves other aspects of your life, then simply change headings for the segments as is appropriate to make the segments of your journey relevant to what you will be working on.

Once you have completed your wheel, use it to help you plan your journey. It's really worth repeating the exercise at regular intervals as you move towards your overall destination as it will show your progress in each area and so highlight your successes and those areas which might be taking longer than you expected to achieve. Once you have that information, you'll know whether you need to amend your route or put extra time and energy into a particular segment of it.

The Wheel of Life

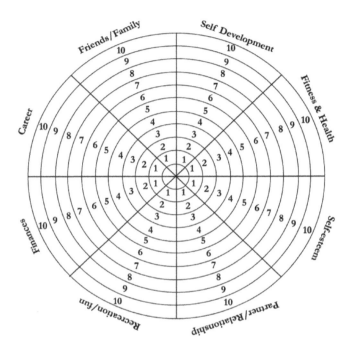

Instructions

Mark each of the segments in the wheel from 0 to 10* to indicate how satisfied you are with that aspect of your life at the moment.

This will indicate to you where to make adjustments and also show how balanced (or otherwise) your life is at the moment.

*0 = completely dissatisfied

10 = completely satisfied

The Wheel of Business

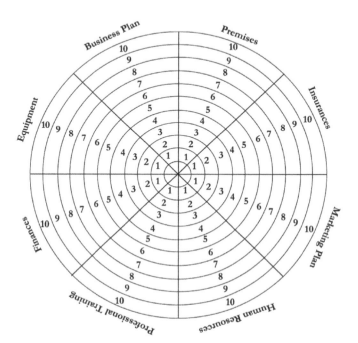

Instructions

Mark each of the segments in the wheel fro to 10* to indicate how prepared you are with that aspect of your business project at the moment.

This will indicate to you where to invest your time and resources and also show how balanced (or otherwise) your overall business plan is at the moment.

*0 = completely dissatisfied

10 = completely satisfied

Activity

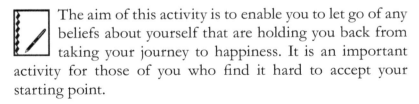 The aim of this activity is to enable you to let go of any beliefs about yourself that are holding you back from taking your journey to happiness. It is an important activity for those of you who find it hard to accept your starting point.

PART ONE: Like the earlier activity, it starts with asking yourself a question and simply noting down the answers that come into your mind.

The question to ask yourself is:

"What do I need to accept, without judgement or regret, in order to set out from where I am now?"

Make a note of anything that occurs to you – some things might be current, others might come from your past.

Once you have your answers, you are ready to move on to part two of this activity - the process of acceptance.

PART TWO: In this part of the activity you will be sending a powerful message to yourself that you are absolutely ready to start your journey – from exactly the place that you are in life right now. This activity will help you to develop complete acceptance of yourself and your current situation at the start of your journey.

To do this, simply repeat the following statements, in the manner described, first thing in the morning and last thing at night, each day for at least two weeks:

1. Stand facing a mirror (head and shoulders only, if you prefer) and look yourself in the eye and smile. Really, genuinely smile warmly, and with compassion.

2. Say to your reflection:

   "I accept you completely for who you are, for all you've been through and for all you've done. Without judgement or regret"

3. Then say:

   "I accept me completely for who I am, for all I've been through and for all I've done. Without judgement or regret"

4. Smile at yourself whilst looking yourself in the eyes again (and wink if you're inclined to!).

Note: The eye contact with yourself is important. Also important is that you use both "you" and "I". This communicates to yourself both internally; as you experience yourself, and externally; as you see yourself in the mirror.

⇝⇝⇝⇝⇝⇝⇝

Whichever aspect of your life you feel isn't quite right, the point to remember is that, no matter what has happened or will happen, you can decide how you will react to it now. You could choose to react in a way which is self-destructive or in a way which will take you further towards where you want to go. Remember - every moment you have the chance to make a decision to live your life differently. Every day you can decide to do something differently, to challenge and change your beliefs if necessary, to find a way to live life which truly satisfies you. So whether it's your career, your finances, your relationships or even where and how you live that you want to change, taking control of your life – getting into the driver's seat – is the place to start.

A glance in the rear view mirror

In this chapter, you have learned how to become the driver of your own life and have looked at why acceptance of your current situation is essential if you are to start off on your journey from the right place. In summary, you have:

- considered whether you have previously blamed external factors for your situation, whether circumstances or other people.

- looked at how taking responsibility for the decisions and choices made as an adult could place you firmly back in control of your own life, and of your future success and happiness.

- learned how luck is actually about how you see the world, based on your beliefs about it.

- learned that you can increase the number of opportunities you notice and take advantage of these by changing your beliefs about the world.

- Considered whether you have been waiting to be able to start from somewhere other than your situation now.

- Learned why accepting you're here and now is vital to a successful journey.

- Started a powerful affirmation of acceptance to ensure you are starting your journey from your current situation, not burdened by regrets and judgements about it.

CHAPTER 2: CHOOSING YOUR DESTINATION

You are now in the driver's seat and ready to start out from your here and now. Before you do set off though, you first need to know exactly where you are going.

In this chapter, you will discover your destination and become more familiar with it. Knowing in detail what your personal happiness and success look like will help you to understand what you need to do to achieve them. You will spend time using your own imagination to learn how it will feel to have achieved just what you want from life. Once you know where you are going, you will be ready to plan the best route for you to get there.

In this chapter, you will also learn the best way to phrase what it is you want from your future – that is, to phrase it in a way that encourages your mind to be open to opportunities to move you onwards. Through these activities, you'll set your destination firmly into your mind, making arriving there inevitable.

Do you know where you're going to?

You probably started out with your dream – your destination – being quite vague. You might have a single phrase to sum up your ambition such as *"I want to be richer"* or *"I want more spare time"*. Some of you might have something a little more definite such as *"I want to retire to the coast"* or *"I want to run my own business"*. It is quite usual for our dreams and ambitions to lack detail. However, if we don't add that detail early on, we risk either not getting to exactly where we want to be or we risk going to somewhere which doesn't really suit us after all. As with any important journey, it is vital that you know exactly where you are going before you start off.

The purpose of this chapter is to work out exactly what you want your future to be – to convert your overall dream into a clear vision of your ideal future. That is, to get a really detailed description of your destination. Once you've done that, you can set out knowing that you really are heading in the right direction.

Be positive

The way in which you phrase your goals influences the likelihood of achieving them. Many people, when asked about their goals, start by giving a list of things that they don't want, such as:

"I don't want to be overweight"

"I don't want to have to worry about money"

"I don't want to feel like a failure"

"I don't want to be lonely anymore"

While that's understandable – after all, we are often motivated in the first instance to move away from anything which makes us uncomfortable, or which causes us distress – it's actually not very helpful. The problem with focusing on what you don't want is that it doesn't tell your mind anything useful about what you do want. The part of your mind that can actually bring about change, the part that drives your behaviours, your decisions, and your habits, isn't given any information about what it needs to do differently to improve your situation.

Would you set out on a car journey in this way? Just imagine getting into your car, switching on your satnav and inputting your desired destination as "not here". If you were to do that, then you could head off in any direction and travel forever without ever reaching a single place that you actually liked and wanted to be. After all, "not here" isn't necessarily a better place than here.

When you set your life goals in terms of what you *don't* like about your life at the moment, you are effectively setting your mind's satnav to *"not here"*.

A common example of this occurs when people decide they hate their job. They focus on getting away from their current job without really working out what they would really love to do for work instead. As a result they find that they move from job to job never really enjoying any position. They are always focussing on *getting away* from a job they dislike, rather than focusing instead on *moving towards* a job they'd love. It is only by knowing exactly where we want to be that we can start to take the journey to get there.

Activity

In this activity, you will begin to identify your destination more clearly, understanding more about your vision of your ideal future. This begins the process of setting your mind's satnav to guide your journey.

PART ONE: This activity also starts with a question to ask yourself. Don't worry if your initial answer is quite broad and vague - as you go through the rest of this activity, you will add more and more detail, eventually getting a clear vision of what you really want for your future. **This vision is the destination of your journey to happiness.**

As you learned above, the key to this activity is not simply what you answer in response to the question - it is *how* you answer it. The wrong type of answer can cause you to become more and more lost on your journey. So let's start...

As before, as you ask yourself this question jot down any answers that come into your mind.

The question is:

"What exactly do I want to achieve?"

PART TWO: Once you have your answers, look through them and highlight any that describe what you *don't* want. Then re-word the highlighted answers so that they describe something that you do want. There are some typical examples of this in the table below:

Original	Possible positive meanings
"I don't want to be overweight"	I want to fit into size x clothes
	I want to feel more energetic
	I want to feel more confident
	I want to be more mobile
	I want to have a healthy BMI of 25
"I don't want to have to worry about money"	I want to earn £x,000 per annum
	I want to be debt free
	I want to be able to save £xy per month
"I don't want to be lonely anymore"	I want to socialise more
	I want some close friends
	I want a wider network
	I want a partner in life

(Template available from: www.gettingyouthere.co.uk/life-in-the-driving-seat/resources).

Once all of your answers are about what you do want, you are ready to move on to the next part of this activity.

PART THREE: In this stage you will be taking some time to daydream about your goals and to create a vision of exactly the future you are aiming for. It's worth taking some time to do this because identifying your destination as specifically as possible is a vitally important step in your journey to the life you want.

You might be unused to using your imagination in this purposeful way, so here are a few steps that can help you get the most out of this activity:

- Find some time when you can be alone and where you won't be disturbed – some people find they daydream best when walking, others while sitting – choose whatever suits you best.

- Imagine how your life will be when you achieve the success and happiness that you want. Really imagine yourself living your ideal life. Make your daydream vivid. Notice what you like best about this daydream – is it a sense of achievement? Or of freedom? Or security? Allow yourself to really imagine the perfect life and learn from your daydreams what you are aiming for. What is it that you actually want?

- Here are some questions to ask yourself about your daydreams:

- Where are you living? Notice the quality of light and the atmosphere

  What are you wearing? How do your clothes make you look and feel?

  What sounds do you hear?

What are people saying to you? How does that make you feel?

How do you feel emotionally?

How do you feel physically?

How do you stand? Practise standing this way – how does it feel?

How do you sit? Practise sitting this way– how does it feel?

How do you walk? Practise walking this way– how does it feel?

What is your facial expression? Practise looking this way– what emotions does it create?

Each time you have a realisation about what it is that you really want, write it down. You will soon have the details you need to be sure of where you are going on your journey. Really understand the answers to those questions you have asked yourself about your dreams – and begin to identify just what they mean to you.

This is not something that you need to do in one sitting. You might spend some time each day over a few days or even weeks. Even after this activity, you might find yourself re-visiting this activity throughout your journey, refining your knowledge of what you want in your life.

ৰ ৰ ৰ ৰ ৰ ৰ

While you're imagining your ideal future, you might find that some parts of your daydreams seem like pure fantasy. That's fine – they are still telling you something about the destination you want to go to. For example, maybe you dream of living on an island. That could be telling you that you want more privacy. Or that you long to be near the coast. Perhaps it's about living in a better climate. A particular image or situation will mean different things to different people, so allow yourself to feel just what each part of your daydreams actually represents to you – what information does it give you about your destination?

Continue daydreaming and really get to know the destination you have chosen. Become really familiar with what it will be like to have achieved your dream – to live that life.

Using your imagination to vividly create a model of the outcome you are seeking allows you to rehearse living that life, and to get a taste of the rewards that await you there. Once you have this, it's time to move on to part four.

PART FOUR: Once you have a vision of what you want for your future, you can start to get specific. For example, if one of the things you have identified as important is "more balance" then really think about what that means. What does balance mean to you? Is it between work and relaxation? Maybe it's about family versus personal time? It will mean different things to different people, so really think about what it means for you. Be specific about what you mean by more too – do you mean a certain number of hours spent doing more or less of a particular activity, or do you mean adding in activities which are completely new (and if the latter, how often and for how long)? When do you want or need to achieve your goal? Adding this level of detail will make your goal more real and will set your mind's satnav more accurately. Being specific also helps you later when you start to plan your route there.

ન્ય ન્ય ન્ય ન્ય ન્ય ન્ય ન્ય

By really knowing and understanding exactly what you mean by success and happiness, and what it would be like to live having achieved them, you can set your destination precisely. Just like when you set your car's satnav to your exact destination, setting your personal destination in this way makes your arrival there inevitable. Of course, you might come across diversions, hold-ups and the odd puncture along the way, but because the destination is set and you know exactly where you are going, you'll always find the way back to your route. At each decision point, you will find that you start to automatically choose the right way for you. That is to say, your decisions, behaviours and thoughts will become naturally aligned to your route.

Develop your own driving style

Your definitions of happiness and success will be unique to you. The activity you have just completed will have created a vision that is uniquely yours. It is therefore important that, throughout your journey, you stay true to yourself. It is vital that you live your life in accordance with your values — anything else will feel uncomfortable in a way that will prevent you from being truly happy. If you feel that something you are doing isn't quite right, doesn't fit with who you really are or what you really want from life, it will eventually derail you.

In order to achieve success on your own terms, you may need to rediscover yourself and your values. Not in a selfish or arrogant way, just in a way which recognises that your own needs and views are valid and that the opinions of others are based on their perspectives and on the life experiences that they have had. Regaining and building self-esteem through this work can free you from self-imposed limitations and enable you to be yourself, and to achieve the things you really want to in life.

Understanding your own values and the beliefs around them can be key to achieving success which has previously seemed out of reach. You will look more closely at this later, when you are asked to think about ways in which you might have previously sabotaged your attempts at success.

You have now identified your destination – your vision. In the next chapter, you will learn how to plan the best route between where you are starting from and your destination. You will also discover that the way in which you word and record your goals within that vision can have a positive impact on your likelihood of achieving each one of them.

A glance in the rear view mirror

In this chapter, you have:

- learned to phrase your goals and dreams in a positive way to make it clearer to you as to what you want to achieve.

- vividly imagined how it will be to live the life you want.

- added specifics to your goals.

- created your clear vision of the life you want

- started to think about your personal driving style.

CHAPTER 3: PLANNING YOUR JOURNEY

In this chapter, you will start to plan your route to your happiness and success. Some of you might have a history of failed plans in the past – but their failure might have been because you hadn't really acknowledged your starting point or clearly identified your destination. Now that you have both of those places pinned down, planning the route from one to the other becomes as exciting as taking the journey itself.

Preparing to travel

It can be tempting, once you've decided where you're going, to rush headlong into a new lifestyle. The trouble is, it's then not long before you feel disappointed when the results aren't immediate or when you realise that your plans didn't take into account the ups and downs of life. All too often, the result is a loss of optimism and motivation and a reversion back to old habits - often even before you've even got off the drive! Therefore, let's take time to think about the journey as well as the destination.

Preparing for your journey enables you to become familiar with the route you are going to take, making sure that you include the major points of interest. It also prepares you to deal with any events that happen along the way. Knowing the best route to your destination, and being aware of alternative routes, if needed, means that you will continue to travel towards your destination, whatever happens.

As you're planning your route, you will also think about how you will reward yourself for your progress and how you will celebrate your successes. You will also learn what motivates you and how to ensure that you can harness the best form of that motivation, so that you keep moving towards your destination of success and happiness.

Think of the literal journeys you make. When you have to go somewhere new for something important, how do you approach getting there? I suspect you take the following steps:

- find out exactly where the place is;
- think about the best way of making the journey - car, train, walking, etc.;
- find out how long the journey will take (and add on a bit for delays and detours);
- gather anything you need to take with you;
- make sure you have enough resources – petrol, cash, food and drink, etc.;
- know who to call if you get delayed and/or need help on the way;

- become familiar with alternative routes and methods of travel in case your original route is blocked in some way.

These basic steps ensure that you can be certain that you'll arrive in the right place, prepared and at the expected time. They are also the same steps that will ensure your success on the journey to achieving the life you want to live.

Yet when we plan to "go" somewhere different in our life – a new career, a new lifestyle, a healthier future - we often forget all about these basic steps and, instead, simply head off with no more than a vague notion about our destination, let alone anything about the route we need to take to get there.

All too often, on deciding that we want something different, we don't spend any time planning on the best way to get it. We chop and change our chosen method to get there. We expect the journey to happen overnight while allowing it to take forever and we expect to make the journey with no/little investment of our resources. Often, we don't even tell anyone what we're aiming to do because we're worried it will fail or be seen as silly, so we have no-one to support us. Finally, we give up the first time our path is blocked or our progress is slowed.

This time, you can avoid each of these pitfalls and set out towards your success confident that you'll get there. These steps to reach a destination successfully are key for achieving any goal. Once you think of achieving your vision of success and happiness as a journey, it's easy to understand the steps needed to make it happen. So, even if you've started out before and failed to get very far, you can now use the above information to make your next journey successful.

Remember, each moment is an opportunity to choose to take your personal journey.

The changes that occur when you are confident that you're on the right journey, and the transformation that achieving success on your own terms brings about, are some of the greatest rewards possible. They enrich you as an individual and as a contributor to your world. So why not start out on that adventure today?

Planning your route

Now that you have your vision and have considered the things that you need to make the vision a reality, you are ready to map out your route to get there. This route is your plan for success and happiness.

Your plan will include all of the things that you have to achieve in order to turn your vision into reality. To achieve your vision you will need to identify individual **goals** which need to be achieved on the way. For example, if you have a **vision** of running your own business, one of your **goals** might be to accumulate a certain amount of money

On the route to achieving each goal, you might have several stages – these are your **milestones.** Using the above example, if the amount of money you need to accumulate to meet your goal is considerable, then you could mark your progress by having **milestones** of every £500 you invest into it along the way. Figure 1 shows you how this might look, and includes a couple of other goals and relating milestones that are commonly part of people's plans.

Your plan will also include the ways in which you will achieve each milestone and goal. Just like working out your vision, the more you can imagine successfully doing what you need to for each goal, the more focus you will have and the more often you will find opportunities to achieve the goal.

It is helpful to also add any dates that are important in your plan. For example, if one of your goals is to train in a new skill, then the dates of enrolment and completion of training courses will need to be in your plan and will influence the earliest date by which you can expect your vision to become reality. Setting a date for achieving your overall vision is also a good idea – even if there needs to be some flexibility around it. If you know when you want to be living in that vision, then you can use that date to work back from it in order to calculate the target dates for each of the various goals and milestones leading up to it.

A simplified example of a plan is shown in the figure below – notice how the milestones build into the goals, which lead to your overall vision of success.

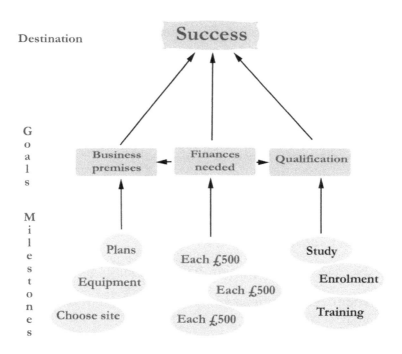

Activity

 You've identified your destination and starting point in the previous chapters, and are now ready to start planning the route between the two. This is your plan for success.

As described above, on the route between your here and now and your destination, there will be the achievements you make along the way as you progress. Each one of these achievements is a goal within your plan. For many of the goals you might also have markers of your progress – milestones – that you can also include in your plan.

The following steps will help you identify and record your goals in a way that will increase the likelihood of your success by making them clear, rewarding and time-focused. These steps will enable you to develop your route to the future that you want:

1. **Write down each goal clearly and specifically,** in as much detail as possible. You should feel excited at this stage (if you're not, then ask yourself if this really is your goal or whether it is something that you believe is what someone else expects of you).

2. **Identify your reasons** for wanting to achieve each goal. The more reasons you have, the stronger your motivation and the better your chance of achieving the goal (more on this in the next chapter).

3. Decide on a **completion date** for your goal.

4. **Identify the actions** you will need to take to achieve your goal.

5. Turn your list into **a plan** by grouping similar activities together in order of priority.

6. **Write down your reward** (big or small) for each activity or milestone that you complete.

A simple way of making a note of these goals, milestones and rewards is to use a table like that shown below (you can download the template from www.gettingyouthere. co.uk/life-in-the-driving-seat/resources). The wording in this table has been carefully chosen to reflect the fact that you are not only imagining yourself achieving each goal and milestone, but you are already identifying how you will achieve it too.

Goal	Watch me...	To do this I'll...	When:	Benefit
1				
2				
3				
4				
5				

Notice how the table also requires you to set a target date for each separate achievement? This is so that you can plan your journey in the right order and ensure that you are progressing along your journey at the speed that you want to. This table is also a place where you can write down the benefits of achieving each of your goals to give you a reminder of your motivation for this journey.

There will inevitably be times when you are waiting for a result or a response with regard to one particular goal and, without something else to work on in the meantime, this can be frustrating and demotivating for some. For this reason, it can be helpful to set goals in each of those aspects of your life that you identified through your Wheel of Life exercise as needing some attention. This will then enable you to be able to maintain your enthusiasm when you have a delay in the progress of your main goal.

Your plan versus your vision

People sometimes confuse the plan with the *vision*. This can lead to people thinking that having alternative strategies (*a plan B*) shows lack of commitment. This is a dangerous error to make, and leads many people to fail in reaching their goal. Remember: your **vision** is the destination, your **plan** is the route you take to it. Sometimes a particular route might be blocked or might no longer exist. Without having considered alternative routes, you could then be completely blocked, or at least severely delayed, in achieving your vision. However, if you have researched the alternative routes, you will still be able to get to your destination successfully.

Identifying alternative routes

There will inevitably be times when the direct route to your destination isn't available. Along the way you might encounter diversions and hold-ups and, occasionally, the road might seem to be blocked. Such events are only a problem for those who haven't thought ahead and identified the alternative routes that are available. That's what you're going to do now. By thinking about what those blockages might be, you can actually plan to deal with them in a way which simply requires a diversion that will still get you to your destination. This is NOT the same as worrying about them. On the contrary, we tend to worry about the things that we feel unprepared for, that we think might ruin everything. By carrying out a realistic risk assessment, and planning what you would do instead, gives you the confidence to know that you are prepared and can handle events, whatever happens along the way.

For example, when you are planning a literal journey which is time critical to an interview or a flight, you probably automatically consider that the journey might take longer than usual due a diversion or other hold-up. In this case, you would familiarise yourself with alternative routes, or start out earlier, or even plan to travel the day before and stay over. The degree to which you plan an alternative depends upon (a) the likelihood of the risk happening and (b) the amount of impact it will have if it does. This process of identifying possible hold-ups and planning for them is standard in business project planning. It is rare, however, for people to do this when planning for personal achievements – and that's a common reason for the failure of personal goals. It is a really valuable step and not only ensures that you get to your destination successfully, it also significantly reduces your level of anxiety whilst travelling there. Your next activity helps you begin this process.

Activity

As you saw above, when planning your journey, it's important to be aware of any challenges and hazards that could crop up on the way. That way you can plan in advance on how to deal with these should they arise. Through this activity, you will become aware of the possible diversions and hold-ups on the way to achieving the life you want and you will plan some alternative routes to take should they occur.

Note: This is not about thinking about the worst-case scenarios. It is about identifying things that have a relatively high likelihood of happening and then simply planning how you will still stay on course, if and when they do.

The table on the next page is an example of a method you can use to enable you to:

- note down any possible hold-ups or diversions that could occur during your journey to your goal.

- identify what you will do to make sure that, should the blockage happen, you have a way of staying on track.

Like your plan, this is a living document which you review every month or so – removing items that are no longer relevant and adding any new items.

Stage of plan	Possible blockage	What to do instead
Taking first steps to start my own business	Friends might not be supportive of my goal and so demotivate me	Join networking group to meet others who are doing or have done the same. Invest in a personal coach to keep you motivated and on track.
Beginning to write my first book	Become isolated while writing and so lose motivation	Join a local writer's group or writing class.
Gain additional qualification	Requires more time to study than estimated	Research different ways the course is offered – do any allow more time? Review timetable – could you fit in extra time in lunch breaks or mornings, for example?

(Template available from: www.gettingyouthere.co.uk/life-in-the-driving-seat/resources).

Knowing that you have considered how to handle likely diversions means you can make your journey with confidence and without fear of getting lost or having to turn back.

It's worth repeating the earlier note: **this is not about thinking about the worst-case scenarios, but identifying things that have a relatively high likelihood of happening and simply planning how you will still stay on course, if and when they do.**

Planning comfort breaks

When thinking about your vision and planning your route, did you ever consider how you might reward yourself for achieving your milestones and goals along the way? Throughout your journey, it's vital that you recognise and reward the progress you're making. After all, you're taking this journey to achieve something worthwhile, so each step closer to your destination deserves to be celebrated. So, have some fun thinking about how you will do this in ways that are both motivational and enjoyable.

Not everyone finds this an easy thing to do. You might even find that both recognising and celebrating your own success feels a little uncomfortable at first – as if to do so is being smug or self-congratulatory in a bad way. It really isn't – it's simply about recognising the efforts and achievements that you are making as you progress. Rewards reinforce the importance of the journey you are making and are a recognition of just how far you have come. They are the rest-stops and comfort breaks along the way, providing light relief and a chance to top-up your enthusiasm and motivation. For these reasons, it's good to recognise that you deserve rewards and then you can have fun building them in to your plan.

For most people, the first step in this process is to accept that – yes, *you do deserve rewards.* Rewards have been shown to be essential when it comes to making successful changes in your behaviour, in particular by changing unhelpful habits (including unhelpful thinking patterns) to more beneficial ones. Rewards send powerful signals to your subconscious to say that your new habits are worthwhile and enjoyable and that you are a success. They remind you that you are achieving what you want to achieve. These signals then encourage your new habits and successful behaviours to continue. Regularly rewarding yourself perpetuates this cycle. Therefore, make sure you are planning plural "rewards".

Don't plan just one big reward at the end - include rewards for your goals and milestones along the way too. Your journey, if made in the best way for you and in a way that is for life, is likely to take some time. Waiting until the final stage of your plan before you recognise the many achievements you have made along the way is depriving yourself of the opportunity to celebrate the success of the various stages along the way, and to reinforce the successful behaviours that have got you so far. Small rewards for the milestones on the way are at least as important as a major reward at the end of the journey - especially for longer journeys when the end of the journey might feel like enough of a reward in itself.

Don't worry about frequent rewards being an expensive habit – they needn't be extravagant or even things which cost much money at all. They can be simple things, which you will really enjoy experiencing and yet rarely make the time to do or have: For example:

- an afternoon relaxing in the garden.
- paperback (or Kindle) book you've been meaning to read.
- coffee with a friend at your favourite cafe.

To be really effective, a reward should be something that you will genuinely enjoy and yet wouldn't just get/do anyway. Your rewards should also be something that will leave you still feeling good about yourself and your achievements – so avoid anything which might make you feel regretful (for example, a food treat if your goal is weight loss, or something expensive that you can't really afford).

Rewards are not only for those milestones that you identified in your plan – they can be for changes in behaviour that you feel proud of too – such as noticing that you have confidence in a situation which would have previously caused anxiety. So be prepared to give yourself some spontaneous rewards too. Once you start thinking about rewards, you'll find that are lots of reasons to reward yourself and to celebrate each step of your journeys.

Activity

 For this activity, you will need the goal-setting sheet you used earlier.

PART ONE: Look at your milestones and goals and the dates you have for each. Then start planning the rewards that you will give yourself on completion of each one. Plan your rewards to be in proportion to the achievement.

Be aware of any rewards that require some advance planning – will you need to get a date in your diary to order your reward or to arrange that coffee with a friend? Planning your rewards at this stage makes it more likely you will actually take them. Otherwise, you might find they take too much time to organise and end up not really feeling connected to the event that you are celebrating.

Write down each reward on your plan and keep your chart where you will see it frequently.

You might also find it helpful to place reminders of the rewards that you are working your way towards around you (photographs, quotations, whatever works best). These will act as triggers to your mind to keep you thinking, feeling and acting in ways that support achievement of your goals.

Imagine what it will be like to get each reward – create a strong mental image with colour, sound and feelings. Do this as often as possible and make it as vivid as possible. This gets your brain 'familiar' with achieving success and becomes motivated to work hard to go for it!

PART TWO: Make a second list of some small rewards that you could have in order to reward yourself for those times when you realise you've achieved a success you might not have even been expecting!

A word of caution

Although your plan is essential, it does not need to be 100 per cent complete before you set off. For some people, the attempt to make their plan perfect gets in the way of ever setting out. Be aware if you start to procrastinate or start looking into minute details for each step. It is quite safe to set out knowing you will still need to do some research into some parts of your route, your plan is a living thing – you will be reviewing and revising it as necessary as you travel along. The important thing is that you have identified where you are going, the main parts of your route, and the places you'll need to visit along the way. After that – it's all about enjoying the trip!

Packing for the journey

When planning your journey, make a list of what you will need to make the most of your destination. Be realistic about what you need and whether or not you currently have it. Some of the things you need will be general and needed wherever you're going. Other things could be specific to you and your goal. This stage may require a bit of time spent planning and researching the options, especially if your plan is an ambitious one. It's well worth spending the time necessary to do this well, as it will save a great deal of time later.

For example, if your journey is to a new career, you might want or need to invest in yourself by training in a new skill or studying a new subject. Consider the various ways available to achieve the outcome you want. Research not only the course or qualification itself - also look into other factors such as the level of financial resources required and the time commitment needed. Nowadays there are a whole range of different ways to learn - through attendance, online, or a combination of the two methods. Therefore, you can find the method of study which fits best into your current responsibilities and enables you to continue earning, if necessary. Be realistic and accept that, for ambitious goals in particular, achieving goals might involve changing your priorities, and will certainly require commitment and flexibility. However, once you can focus on the long-term benefits and end results, you are likely to realise that it becomes acceptable to make short-term sacrifices and each step you take towards your vision will motivate you to continue.

Activity:

In this activity, you will be thinking about what you need for your journey and check that you have them in place or, at least, that you know where you will get them when you need them. One way to work out what you need; you can carry out what I call the "F-TEST" to discover what you'll need on your journey. F-TEST stands for: Finances, Training, Environment, Support and Time.

Preparing well for your journey will enable you to set off with confidence and to have a realistic expectation of the journey ahead. Of course, there are likely to be some unexpected events along the way, but by being aware of what you need, enables you to plan your finances, time and time-scales realistically and will make the journey much more enjoyable.

So grab your pen and paper again, read through each part of the F-TEST and note down your answers and thoughts for each part of it. Also, note which things you will need in place at the outset, and which things you can get when at the relevant point in your journey.

The F-TEST

F – Finances. Do you have the funding you need for your project? If not, have you got plans in place to get it? Getting the finance needed for your journey could be one of your goals. If it is a considerable amount, then you might also have milestones at each £100 or £1,000 saved, or of securing finance if that is what is needed.

T – Training. Do you need additional skills or knowledge? This could be directly related to your vision, or it might be indirectly connected. For example, if your vision is to become self-employed, do you need training in marketing or basic business administration?

E – Environment. Where will you work on the changes you want to make? Do you need a quiet place to study? Perhaps you need business premises or storage space? If you have a fitness goal, where will you focus on your physical training?

S – Support. Who will help you along your way? You might need support and advice from professionals in order to achieve your goals. You might need practical support such as childcare or pet care while you do your training. You will certainly benefit from friendship and moral support along the way.

T- Time. When will you spend time on your plan, working your way towards each milestone and goal? Be realistic about how much time you need and work out how and when you will find that time.

Once you have completed the F-TEST you will know just what you need to make your journey successful. You will have carried out an exercise that greatly increases your ability to set out and complete your journey to the future you want.

Now that you have thought about your destination in life and the resources and changes you need to make to achieve what you want, you can now check that you have all the resources you need to start your journey and really get to where you want to be in life!

A glance in the rear view mirror

In this chapter, you have:

- learned that your route from where you are now to your destination (your vision) is your plan.

- related your journey to success and happiness to other journeys you have made, learning the steps to ensure a successful journey.

- identified the goals and associated milestones within your plan.

- identified goals in each area of your life you want to improve.

- imagined yourself achieving each goal and milestone in order to identify how you will achieve each one.

- planned how to deal with delays and diversions, identifying alternative routes that could be taken, if necessary.

- learned the importance of rewarding and celebrating your progress and successes.

- identified what you will have/do as your reward or celebration for each milestone and goal along the way.

- planned your rewards and celebrations and incorporated them into your plan, and added them to your diary where necessary.

- listed some small rewards you can get when you have small victories and successes that you were not expecting.

- thought about the resources you will need on your journey.

- carried out your own F-TEST to work out what those resources are for you.

PART TWO: Your journey

"The journey between what you once were and who you are now becoming is where the dance of life really takes place"

- Barbara De Angelis

CHAPTER 4: SETTING OFF

As you begin your journey, along with doing a final check to make sure you have all you need to begin, it's useful to also be aware of anything that you might need to pick up along the way. If there are things that you'll need (and there probably will be) then you can make sure that your planned route to your destination includes acquiring them along the way. You can include obtaining each of these things as separate milestones on your plan.

In this chapter, you'll identify the things you need to support you as you travel, along with those things which will be needed to keep you going. From motivation and emotional support to professional advice, these are the things that can make the difference between success and failure. By checking at the start of your journey that you know where to obtain them, you'll make your journey with more confidence.

The best way to stay on course is to check your progress regularly. That way you can make corrections and alterations necessary to your methods before you have deviated significantly off course. In this chapter, you will also learn a way of doing this checking that can easily be fitted into your journey as you go along. That way, you can avoid many of the sort of break-downs and diversions that can occur otherwise.

Indicate before pulling out

I've worked with a number of clients who, having experienced the disappointment of not having achieved their goals in the past, have decided that they want their journey to be a secret. Lack of confidence, fear of disbelief or fear of ridicule has led them to begin their journey alone. Tempting as this might seem, it is not the best way to approach your journey to success. Other people can be a great source of support, motivation and advice. There are bound to be times on your journey when you are tired and demotivated, and times when you're bursting with enthusiasm and pride. In both instances, having someone to express your feelings to, and to share your experiences with, will be a huge advantage. So do let some people know about the journey you are about to embark upon.

Of course, if you know that someone will be dead-set against you, you don't need to involve them. However, the people already in your life who are supportive can really help you on your way. In fact, the morale and practical support of other people will be vital. Getting them on-board at the start can give you a real boost – maybe it's practical help with childcare, looking after pets or simply watering your plants while you train or study; maybe it's as a "critical friend" to sound out your ideas to; or maybe it's a shoulder to lean (or even cry) on when the going gets tough and to celebrate with when things go well. Get yourself a great team around you and your journey will be easier and more enjoyable.

Telling others about what you are about to do also increases your level of commitment and provides a sense of accountability. In fact, one reason people sometimes give for not telling others about their plan initially is that it makes it "too real" and they worry that they are not yet ready to believe in themselves. The very act of broadcasting what you are doing and what you intend to achieve will increase your self-belief, and, as you answer people's questions about your plans, you will find your vision of your future becoming more vivid and more certain in your own mind as well as in theirs.

Fuel up and keep moving

To stay inspired and motivated about your goals and to keep travelling towards them no matter what, your motivation needs to come from within yourself. You need to discover your intrinsic motivation – that motivation which is independent of external factors. This is the fuel that provides you with the energy and enthusiasm for your journey. Even if you are also motivated by something external such as money or the approval of others, unless you can find something within yourself that motivates you irrespective of those things, your chances of success are not at the maximum. Studies have shown that people who succeed are those who are making a change that **they want for themselves.** They're not doing it for someone else, even though others might benefit, and they are not doing it because they feel they ought or should. That is, they have strong intrinsic drivers.

Common intrinsic motivators include:

- striving for personal excellence.
- a desire to develop a particular recreational or professional skill.
- the desire to be able to live independently.
- a passion for a specific cause.

Intrinsic motivation provides your own drivers. They are there even during the times when no one is expressing their approval, and even when there is no monetary gain. They exist as motivators in and of themselves, and so are strong and permanent. These are the motivators that will keep you going during the tougher parts of the journey, ensuring that you continue to your destination.

Activity

Think about the things which are motivating you to take this journey. Make a note of them and keep them in the forefront of your mind. Highlight the ones which are not dependent on someone else – those which come completely from yourself. Write out each one of these on a separate piece of paper or card and pin them up somewhere you will see them each day.

ৡৡৡৡৡৡৡ

Are we there yet?
Checking your route and travel time

As with all journeys we make, there is a risk that sometimes we will take a wrong turning and end up travelling in the wrong direction or end up stuck in a dead end. Regularly checking that you are still on your route will allow you to quickly spot any wrong turns you might have taken. The process of reviewing and adjusting need not be a source of stress and can simply be a routine part of your journey. The process is shown in the diagram on the following page:

For example, if you are aiming to lose weight, then regular weighing and measuring will enable you to know if the techniques you are using are working or not. Noticing that you have gained 1 or 2 pounds of weight over two weeks in a row will signal to you that you need to change something. It will be much easier then to get back on track as your deviation will be small. However, if you were not weighing yourself regularly, it might take until you have gained several more pounds before you notice, by which time you have a much bigger adjustment to make and a longer delay before you are back on track.

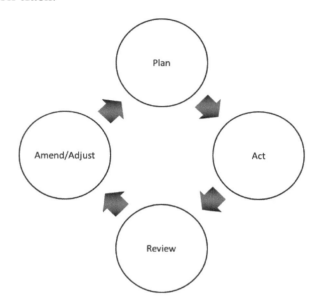

As with the rest of this journey, there is no benefit to feeling guilty or regretful if you find that you have not been progressing as well as you thought towards one of your goals or milestones. Remember: **all results are simply feedback on what you have been doing** and lack of progress is a lesson about your current methods.

Another common area in which this occurs is when people decide to become home-based for work. Some people doing this find they cannot maintain focus on their work and decide that perhaps they are not suited to working from home. However, reflecting on what's actually happening in their thoughts and behaviours often reveals that simple changes to the way they arrange their working day can make a big difference. Some find they need a routine and, if they create a timetable for their work, they can maintain a work-like approach at home. Others find that they need a way of separating home life from work life; one client found that he could do this by starting his morning with a "walk to work" – walking around the block and entering a work mind-set as he walked back in through his front door and then doing a similar "walk home" at the end of his working day. He was a great illustration of how home/work separation can be a mental exercise as well as a physical one. It also demonstrates how reviewing a plan can reveal small amendments that can be made to improve your rate of progress.

Checking your wheels

To check on your overall progress, every so often, re-visit the Wheel of Life (or Wheel of Business) that you completed at the start of your journey (p.16) and assess whether you are progressing in all of the areas that you wanted to change. To do this, simply take a fresh copy of your wheel template and complete it again. Notice how far you've travelled in each area and make any adjustments.

If your journey is a long one, you can do this regularly and compare each new one to your earlier ones. Seeing your wheel expand and become more balanced is a real motivator in itself – and cause for one of those rewards that you've planned.

A glance in the rear view mirror

In this chapter, you have:

- considered your need for support from others – professional, practical and emotional.

- uncovered your intrinsic motivation, which will keep you going towards your destination even if things get tough.

- learned how to monitor and review your plans.

- learned the importance of spotting deviation from your route quickly.

- discovered how you can use your Wheel of Life/ Business to get an overview of your progress to your new life.

CHAPTER 5: SILENCING THE BACK-SEAT DRIVER

When travelling along on your journey, you might experience episodes of negative self-talk. At times, the voice in the back of your head might be sceptical about your ability to succeed. You might hear it doubting your purpose, your direction and even whether you deserve the success you're aiming for. It might criticise your route and might even question your destination itself.

In this chapter, you will discover some ways of silencing that voice and the doubts that it can create. You will learn how to stay confident and focused on your milestones, goals and destination instead. You will also learn something about how patterns of failure to achieve your dreams in the past can help you identify how you sabotage your dreams - and what you can do to prevent this from happening again.

Your personal back-seat driver

Do you sometimes experience low self-esteem and poor levels of confidence, even when things are going well for you? Do you ever feel that you are somehow not good enough, that you are lacking in some way? If such negative feelings are getting in the way of your success, then perhaps becoming more aware of your inner dialogue will be a key step toward changing your life for the better.

It is not unusual for people to be so used to their own inner dialogue that they allow it to provide its narrative to their days without censor. However, for many people, that inner dialogue is incredibly self-critical. Often, it is only when you start to consciously listen to that dialogue that you become aware of the negative messages it gives. It's amazing how often our internal critic tells us that we're not good enough - saying such things as *"You're fat", "You're incompetent", "You always fail", "People like you don't get good jobs"* and other such corrosive things.

You might find that it often repeats its limiting beliefs and harsh criticisms over and over again. The result of this is that you are spending your days with an unremittingly critical and judgmental narrative accompanying almost everything you do.

Maybe what's even more amazing about this critical self-talk is how much notice we take of it. The messages it gives you might seem to have been there forever, but are likely to have come from your parents and/or other adults who were around when you were growing up, or it might be things you told yourself when you were just a child without any awareness of your real potential. Wherever your negative beliefs and messages come from, the good news is that you can learn to control and change this dialogue - and make life-changing differences to the way you think, feel and behave.

A good first step towards having a happier and more successful life is to become aware of these negative messages so that you can construct more positive messages to replace them. This is what you will start to do in the next activity.

Activity

 Over the next few days, become aware of any criticisms made by your own inner dialogue. Notice the following things:

- When does the self-criticism start? Does it start the moment you wake up, or is there a particular trigger?

- Does your inner voice criticise one or two particular things, or is it more critical generally?

- Does your critical self-talk exaggerate negative situations by including words such as always or never?

- Can you identify where the criticism comes from? Does it go back to your childhood or adolescence?

One helpful technique in stopping that critical voice is to imagine that it was someone else saying these things to you – a back-seat driver in your life's journey. What would your response to such an insulting, hurtful person be? Hopefully, you would tell the speaker, in no uncertain terms, to shut up and go away. This is exactly what you should do with that critical voice in your head. Don't listen to it, don't argue with it – simply tell it to shut up and then think of something else – anything, even the most mundane thing you can think of, such as your evening meal or a programme that you're currently watching on television. This simple exercise starts to puts you back in control of your self-image and confidence.

Be assured that this activity of initially becoming more aware of your inner critical voice doesn't give the criticisms more power – on the contrary, once you notice what your back-seat driver is saying, you can see the thoughts as simply thoughts and nothing else, and so start to ignore them and let them go.

This awareness gives you the power to change the way you think and to start doing the things you would like to do.

ॐॐॐॐॐॐॐ

As you become more familiar with what that critical inner voice is saying, you can gain control over it. You can then begin to replace it with more positive thoughts by finding exceptions to the criticisms so that the words such as *always* or *never* have no credibility. If you realised that the criticisms came from years back you can recognise the amount of personal growth you have made since then, and you might also realise that the criticism was unfounded and unfair. It might also be that you perceived a criticism in an innocent or misunderstood comment.

Sometimes we are critical of ourselves for a behaviour or habit that we genuinely believe is unhelpful, such as poor time-keeping or unhealthy eating habits. If you find this is the case for you, then include changing these behaviours in your plan. You could set a number of milestones on the way to a goal of being a punctual person or having a healthier lifestyle.

Whatever you discover about your self-dialogue, the act of listening to it will put you back in control. Remember, they are your thoughts and you can choose to think differently. It might take a little time to develop new and positive thinking habits, especially if you have been criticising yourself for a long time. While the negative narrative is allowed to run in the background it is very harmful – it is listened to by your subconscious and taken seriously. Once we switch it off we can then repair our egos and start to rebuild our confidence. Whether the criticisms come from the adults in our past or from television shows and magazines that we grew up paying attention to, it doesn't matter - what matters is that your adult self can silence that voice and start building a much more constructive dialogue with yourself.

The questions we ask ourselves

There is another part of your inner dialogue that has a profound effect upon the way you progress on your journey: the questions that you ask yourself when you are dealing with a particular challenge or problem. In my experience, most people ask themselves questions such as,

"Why am I in this position?"

"Why has this happened to me (again)?"

These questions will tend to result in you becoming stuck in the problem, with decreasing levels of confidence and self-belief. The reason for this is that your mind will do its best to answer the specific question that you have asked it. When your questions are asking for reasons why you are in your current position, the answers will simply be a list of explanations and excuses for why you are where you are. That is to say, the answers will simply focus on the fact that you're not where you want to be. They will not include any information about the way out of your predicament. Such answers won't provide solutions and certainly won't take you forward at all - they will simply reinforce your belief that you're stuck.

A more useful style of question to ask is to phrase as follows:

"What's the best way to get out of this position?"

"How might I change my situation?"

"How could I possibly approach this problem differently?"

These questions are much more helpful. Firstly, they presuppose that you can move forward from the situation you are in. Secondly, they automatically generate answers which are more helpful.

For example, if you are driving along and get a puncture, the first type of question would lead you to asking, *"How did I get this puncture?"* The answers you might come up with might be:

"I drove over a nail" or *"Someone did this while my car was parked".* These sorts of answers still leave you at the side of a road with a puncture.

If, instead you asked yourself, *"How can I best fix this situation?"* Your answers might be:

"I could swap the wheel for the spare"

"I could call out the rescue services"

"I could call a friend who could change the wheel" and so on.

You can see how much more helpful these types of answers are as they are all focused on a solution to your problem.

Activity

To help you develop the habit of asking the more useful type of questions, have the question *"How might I ......?"* written somewhere so you can see it regularly – above your computer, on the bathroom cabinet, in the kitchen, etc.

Developing the habit of asking yourself the second type of questions will get you moving towards your destination faster than you can imagine.

ॐ ॐ ॐ ॐ ॐ ॐ ॐ

Using your imagination well

The impact of our inner dialogue on the way we think, feel and behave is an example of how powerful our imagination can be. Earlier you used your imagination to identify your vision for your ideal future - your destination. In this section, you'll learn more about using your imagination. You will learn how to use it to help you spot all of the opportunities around you, and to guide your decisions and choices in ways that take you nearer to that vision. Good use of your imagination can support you on your journey. Conversely, letting your imagination create bad scenarios can sabotage your journey and make success unlikely. It's worth training yourself to use that powerful imagination of yours to its best.

Do you enjoy daydreaming? Maybe you were told as a child that it was a waste of time - that you should be doing something more productive, more active. I come across many people who say they stopped daydreaming long ago. By this they usually mean that they've stopped imagining wonderful, fantastic adventures or they no longer vividly imagine what it would be like to have their perfect life.

Daydreaming can be a highly beneficial activity. By imagining vividly what success looks like, feels like and sounds like, your mind can become alert for opportunities to achieve it. The result of imagining feeling great, being calm and feeling confident, is that your body responds as if you were those things. As you imagine these things your body posture changes to a more confident one, stress hormones are decreased and confidence hormones increase. You become more likely to take positive actions as you know what it feels like to experience them.

On the other hand, as the imagination cannot be literally turned off, those people who stop daydreaming of the best possible future often take up another form of daydreaming instead, without even realising it. They have taken up what I call "daymaring" - they use their imagination to vividly imagine worst-case scenarios. They imagine that loved ones who are late have been hurt, that every pain is a dread disease, that every interaction will be negative. Not surprisingly, they feel stressed, anxious and have problems sleeping well.

Daymaring is a self-feeding monster. As you imagine fear, grief, anger and upset, your body responds with the fight or flight response that evolved millennia ago to deal with real, acute threats to life. The more this response is activated, the more likely you are to perceive threats around you, which then stimulate the flight and fight response further, and so on. Eventually your physical and mental health suffer due to the chronic state of stress generated by this pattern of thinking.

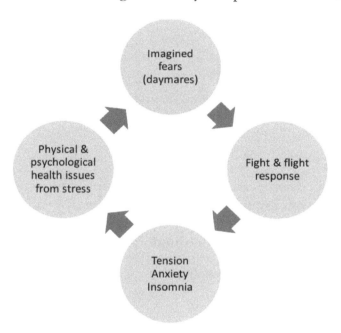

What a tragic waste of imagination! To think of how the imagination can work for us – enabling us to imagine the best of worlds, to plan our successes and to explore the things that would make us happy – and then to use it to frighten ourselves and to make ourselves unwilling to explore and enjoy. How sad.

How much better for your health and well-being to experience the benefits of using your imagination for positive dreams instead:

So do become aware of what you are using your imagination for. Are you using it to keep you in a state of perpetual fear and anxiety or to generate a perpetual state of optimism and motivation? **It's your imagination so you get to choose.**

Excuses and self-sabotage

Excuses

As we have seen, the self-dialogue that accompanies setting out on a new journey can be anything from thoughts of excitement and joy to ones of fear and anxiety. You might hear yourself thinking that you can't make the journey - that you're too old, you have too many commitments, or that you're too unfit. You might therefore feel that it isn't possible to go on your journey because of your situation.

For those of you who feel a long way from where you want to be, it can be helpful to look at others who started from similar positions to you, or whose starting point was far from ideal. Take a look at the examples below for some inspiration:

JK Rowling was an unemployed single mum who believed herself to be a complete failure when she first came up with the idea for her Harry Potter books. She was rejected by 12 publishers before finding one that would publish her book. She is now one the world's best-selling authors and her books have become the basis for some of the biggest blockbuster films ever made. The transformation she made was the result of her determination and passion to write and her perseverance in the face of rejection.

Fauja Singh enjoyed running in his youth, but gave up in his 30s. He started running again when he was aged 84 and, shortly afterwards, participated in international marathons. Aged 93, he achieved a new world record for the over-90s marathon by completing the 26.2 mile distance in six hours and 54 minutes – nearly an hour faster than the previous record and faster than many a fraction of his age would manage. He completed his last marathon just before his 102nd birthday.

Steve Brown had an accident in 2005, which left him paralysed from the chest down. He has described how he felt resentful and desolate as he tried to come to terms with his paralysis. However, he became inspired when watching a game of wheelchair rugby and decided to start training in the sport. In 2011, Steve became captain of the Great Britain Wheelchair Rugby team, leading the team at the 2012 Paralympics. He now works as a television reporter (mainly sport) and as a speaker and mentor. He was voted as a member of the *"2015 Power 100: The most influential people in Britain with a disability or impairment"*.

There are many such accounts of people succeeding despite situations that others would regard as reasons for not even pursuing ambitions. The difference between those that do succeed and those who do not even try, is what they are telling themselves – what they believe about the world and about their abilities. That is, they have focused on their destination, accepted their starting point and have passionately and doggedly stuck to the route they need to take. At each setback they have sought out the opportunities to continue. Through the activities within this book, you are becoming equipped to do the same.

If you are still in doubt about whether someone at your age, or your level of fitness, can achieve an ambitious goal, here are two more examples of how situations previously assumed to work against success are actually no barrier at all:

A study by US military scientists monitored a large number of ex-military personnel for decades after leaving the forces. At the beginning of the study all the men were young and fit. By the age of 60, some had kept themselves very fit and others had not – some had been very inactive and had become very unfit. The researchers then put members of both of these groups through a gruelling exercise boot camp. At the end of the boot camp, those men who had been unfit improved their fitness to become as fit as those who had maintained their fitness throughout. This is a great example of how, even when we feel that we've let ourselves go, or are simply too old, we can still make impressive improvements when we devote ourselves to our goals.

A report by The Global Entrepreneurship Monitor (GEM) UK 2013 Report has found that more people than ever before are starting a business beyond the age of 50. In a separate GEM study it was found that businesses set up by older people have a greater chance of success, with 48% of businesses set up by the over-50s surviving over five years, compared to just 29% of those set up by people aged 18-49.

The Prince's Initiative for Mature Enterprise (PRIME) is a national charity, which supports business creation for the over 50s. Alastair Clegg, Chief Executive of PRIME, said:

*"Everyone is talking about the rise of self-employment and new
businesses being started and this report confirms that it's the over 50s
who are driving this positive trend forward.*

*"The over 50s have the skills, experience and dedication that naturally
lend themselves to enterprise and businesses started by older people help
benefit the economy, provide jobs and work for other people and more
importantly, help keep older people in the workforce."*

Do not let your age be an excuse for not pursuing your dream
– however old (or young) you are, planning for your success
will take you in the right direction.

So, whatever your situation in life, by identifying your passion
and the destination that it could lead you to, you too could
achieve more than you might have even dared to dream in
the past. There might be times when your ambition and
dreams are in danger of becoming overwhelmed by your
finances, your age or your current level of fitness. At those
times, just take a look around at others who have achieved
despite those things. Let yourself be inspired. Know
that, although your exact journey is unique to you, the
obstacles along the way will probably have been overcome
by others – and that you can learn how to overcome them
too. Remember that even the longest road can only be
travelled one mile at a time and, those who have gone along
the road before, have left signposts and directions to guide
you too.

Self-sabotage

Often, when we look back over previous attempts to
achieve the success and happiness we are aiming for, we
can see patterns of behaviour that have caused us to give
up or fail. On reflection, it can often seem that we are our
own worst enemies, always ending up in the same position,
resulting from our own repeated patterns of thinking and
behaviour.

Self-sabotage is often the result of our beliefs about a particular aspect of the goal or vision we are aiming for. If we have always told ourselves something negative about the place we want to get to in life, our subconscious behaviours will act to prevent us from getting there. This might sound odd at first, but once you have realised that your subconscious is simply trying to protect you from something that it believes is bad, it makes more sense.

Here are some common examples of this, which I often come across in clients - you might find they sound familiar to you too:

Sabotaging financial success: beliefs about money can interfere with a person's vision of becoming financially secure and successful in their careers. Those who have grown up believing that people can only make money by taking advantage of others, or through immoral or unethical behaviour, will find they sabotage opportunities to make above a certain amount of money. After all, if you are a good person, and you believe that only bad people become wealthy, then it makes perfect sense for you to subconsciously make sure that you don't become one of those people – that you stay true to yourself.

Sabotaging career progression: a person who has been brought up to believe that all workplaces can be separated into "them" (the bosses) and "us" (the workers), can experience subconscious conflict when the chance to be promoted to a managerial position arises. The belief that they will be leaving the group to which your family and friends belong ("us") to go to "them" can result in behaviours which make sure it never really happens. If, despite this belief, a person with these beliefs does get promoted, then their stress levels might rise until they either resign from the new post, or until they can begin to focus on the next level of management to see as "them" (thus causing similar problems at the next level of promotion).

Sabotaging work:home balance: a person who has a belief that they should work long hours and be seen to be doing so, and who also has strong values around being a present member of their family – requiring them to be present as a parent, sibling or child – is likely to feel torn as to where to spend their time. Whether they are at home or at work they will feel that they should be at the other. As a result, they often find that both their work and personal goals get thwarted by their own sub-conscious behaviours.

Sabotaging overall personal happiness and success: a person who believes that keeping others happy is important, often finds achieving their own dreams difficult, if not impossible. Such people often find that they sabotage personal dreams if someone in their lives is perceived to express disapproval in any way. Their belief that others always come first prevents them investing their time and energy on their own dreams.

Most people are not conscious of these conflicts between beliefs and values. Thinking about patterns of failure to succeed in your ambitions can be a good start to becoming conscious of the beliefs that have been getting in your way. Once you do become aware of those beliefs, you can then start to consider how you might modify them to remove the conflict. For example, do you need to update your beliefs, or do you need to change something about your destination? Realising that you could adapt your belief in tune with your values can help you continue to your chosen destination.

Using the examples above you could:

- focus on earning and investing money ethically, and so remove the conflict which sabotages your earning capacity.

- identify how you could be a fair and hard-working manager, so you can move through your career more comfortably.

- improve your time-management, delegation and other skills so that you work at a high level of productivity within your working hours, whilst prioritising your family in non-working time.

- expressing your care and support to those close to you who care when you are available, whilst setting respectful boundaries, which enables both sides to feel comfortable in saying "no" at times.

Identifying these clashes of beliefs enables you to examine your drivers and behaviours with conscious perspective – a first step towards identifying which beliefs are really important to you, which are less so, and whether any of them are based on out-of-date assumptions and experiences. From there it becomes possible to identify ways that all of your real core values can be met without disrupting progress towards the success you want. You will then be ready to say goodbye to your worst saboteur – you!

The next activity will help you consider previous experiences and patterns, which might suggest that you have a conflict between values and beliefs impacting upon your ability to succeed in your goals. You can then start to address these so that they no longer get in your way.

Activity

One way that you can identify where these clashes of beliefs and vision exist is to think back to your previous attempts to achieve your goals and vision. Can you see a pattern in which you always seem to fail at the same point? You might have blamed external factors at the time, but now think about your role in the failure – did you allow yourself to be late for an interview or fail to prepare as well as you could have? Did you make poor spending or investment choices?

What can you learn from the patterns you identify?

༞༞༞༞༞༞༞

Dealing with road rage

Many of us have people in our life with whom we always seem to clash. Sometimes it's someone who we feel frequently misunderstands us (or you frequently misunderstand them). You might find this problem becomes more noticeable with some people when they learn of your plans. Some might not understand why you want to change your life and others might think that you should do things differently – by which they usually mean do things the way they would.

In this situation, we tend to get frustrated, labelling the other person as "difficult" and knowing that they are thinking the same of us. However, in many cases, such understandings aren't based in the reality of the situation at all. They often result from the fact that the people involved have different ways of communicating and of seeing the world.

Two common examples of this type of disagreement are:

- people who deal with detail and those who take a "big picture" view of situations often find themselves clashing over many topics.

- those who naturally see differences more clearly than similarities often conflict with those for whom similarities are most obvious.

The consequence of such differences is that any points of agreement are often missed. The differences become exaggerated as tempers flare and patience diminishes – sometimes to the point of an impasse forming.

These types of disagreements can be distracting and might even get in the way of your progress. Luckily, when you become aware that there is a pattern of conflict between you and another person, there are some things that you can do to rescue the situation. Then you can move towards a much more productive dialogue with that person.

One useful method of dealing with disagreements is for each person involved to state their overall objective by describing the outcome they want to achieve, instead of arguing about the immediate detail. This approach is helpful because, very often, each person involved will actually want the same or similar outcome. If that's the case, you can then work together to identify the common goals you share. As each person acknowledges the other's perspective, it will enable a better all-round approach to be taken.

During any dispute, be aware that you might each be using the same words to mean different things. I have known whole projects come to a halt because of one team using a lay meaning of a word to a technical team who interpreted it in a very precise way and in a way that made the team's request impossible. Again, be willing to describe what you want the outcome to look like – that way the other side has a chance to understand what you require and so explain any problems, if any, or to realise that they can deliver what is needed.

Finally, remember that there are no mind readers. If you feel you have been misunderstood or are misunderstanding something, be willing to say so. Be willing even to describe in detail which parts of the problem are causing you difficulty – and be willing to listen to the same from the other side. Having a mutual understanding can help both sides review their communication method.

Throughout, remember that opinions should not be confused with facts and that we all have different maps of the world around us – some notice the details and some the overall landscape, some see the technicalities, some the conceptual. All ways are valid and can complement each other. Problems arising from communications styles are commonplace, and recognising and understanding this issue is key to conflict resolution.

Defending of opinions as if they are facts is a major source of conflict. This is particularly the case where the opinion we hold has been held for so long (maybe even "handed down" in our family) that we have never even noticed that it is only an opinion. For example, I will sometimes ask a group of people about the "right" way to store socks. The population generally falls into two camps: those who make a little ball out of each pair, and those who just tuck the tops of pairs together. Both are, of course, entirely valid techniques. However, many members of each group will state categorically that their method is the correct way. They will even offer explanations as to *why* their method is correct. The debate can last a little while and I admit that I enjoy watching the debate unfold.

Of course, there is no "correct" way to store socks - whatever works for you, works and is therefore ok. Yet, because putting socks away is usually something people learn at home when they are very small, it's something which feels like a factual, black-and-white issue. Something about which there is a definite right way to do it. Something for which there is a right answer.

Many of the things we feel are right and for which we argue, are actually simply opinions, beliefs and traditions rather than factual, provable matters. In fact, many breakdowns in communications, even relationships, occur because we mistake opinion as fact.

I once worked with a client who was having constant arguments at home about differences over how different household tasks "should" be done - each person believing that, not only was there a single, correct way to do each task (their way, of course), but that each was worth arguing about. The relationship was suffering because of all these small arguments yet, at the end of the day, all they were arguing about was the equivalent of how to store socks - what a sad waste of an otherwise sound relationship.

Whenever you find yourself in any conflict about something, remember to ask yourself these two questions:

"Is this something which can be proved to be true, in all cases, for all people?"

"Are the consequences of a different approach damaging to anyone or anything?"

If the honest answers are "no" to both questions, then be open to agreeing to disagree. You don't have to change your belief or preference (though you might find you become more willing to compromise), just be more open to accepting that others' views are just as valid as yours, and probably feel just as right to them.

Of course, this isn't to say that you should stop debating or campaigning for the causes you believe in, it just means being able to separate the important stuff (for which one or both of the above questions can be answered with a "yes") from the unimportant. This also supports your self-esteem as it means you learn to see differences as just that, rather than as personal criticisms. Once you can do this, you are less likely to be distracted from your choice of your future and your route to it – able to stay on course to your ideal future whilst accepting and respecting that others might choose a different way.

A glance in the rear view mirror

In this chapter, you have:

- become aware of your inner dialogue and to change it to a more positive one.

- learned about the power of your imagination and how you can harness it to work with you on your journey to success and happiness.

- reflected on how you might be sabotaging yourself and how others might sabotage your journey too.

- learned of others who have succeeded despite external circumstances which others might have seen as obstacles.

- understand common causes of conflict and ways to resolve them.

CHAPTER 6: IN-CAR ENTERTAINMENT

While you're on your journey, you will be able to choose what you have as your entertainment and stimulation. For an exciting journey, that keeps you motivated and on track to your destination, it is wise to choose well. All of the input we have into our brains – the things we read, watch and listen to – are taken notice of by our subconscious, and contribute to the way we see the world and the beliefs we form about it. In turn, these affect our self-esteem, motivation and belief in our ability to achieve success.

In this chapter, you will start to think carefully about the information you feed your subconscious mind – the things which will influence the way you see the world as you travel on your journey. You will learn how the things you input into your mind have a powerful effect on the way you see the world, and how, by choosing these things carefully, you can really improve your confidence, increase your ability to make the most of opportunities and make success inevitable.

GIGO (Garbage in – Garbage out)

There is saying in the fields of computer science: *"Garbage In – Garbage Out".* It means that, because computers simply follow instructions, they will produce unwanted, useless and unhelpful responses if they receive input which is incorrect, unhelpful or nonsensical. A similar process occurs in our brains. If we choose to take in negative, hurtful and cynical messages above all else, we will start to find that we see the world that way. If we choose predominantly to read magazines and newspapers which focus on gossiping and on criticising others, or we mainly watch programmes which revel in the failures and weaknesses of others, then gradually we will not only see the world through these lenses ourselves, but we will also tend to assume that the world views us that way. The negative effects of this can be that:

- your self-esteem and confidence dwindle as you become more self-critical and believe everyone else is judgemental.

- you become blind to the opportunities around you.

- you fail to recognise genuine offers of help as you become more cynical about the motives of others.

- your motivation dwindles.

- you start to feel down and helpless about the journey ahead, and risk giving up.

On the other hand, if you choose your "inputs" well and predominantly read, watch and listen to things which show success, are supportive of people's achievements, and which generate happiness, then the reverse can happen:

- your self-esteem and confidence increase as you see what is possible.

- you notice the opportunities around you.

- you recognise and are able to accept genuine offers of help.

- your motivation increases.

- you feel a sense of happiness, possibility and achievement throughout your journey.

Because of this impact upon our thinking, feelings and behaviours at a sub-conscious level, we are often unaware of their influence upon us. Subconscious changes feel natural and so we simply change without being aware. Therefore, if we set out on our journey whilst continuously exposing ourselves to negative messages, we risk becoming more and more disillusioned, without realising why. The following activity will help you ensure that doesn't happen, and that you stay positive throughout your journey to success.

Activity

This activity is aimed at making you more aware of the sort of inputs you've been giving your mind. It will provide you with the information you need to empower yourself to develop a powerfully positive mind-set.

For this activity, first either draw a table like the one shown opposite or download the template from www.gettingyouthere.co.uk/life-in-the-driving-seat/resources.

Cast your mind back and recall the magazines, newspapers, books, radio programmes and the programmes you have read, listened to or watched over the last month or so. Note each one down in the table, under the heading "Item". Then put a tick (✓) in each column that you think describes some or all of the content of each item:

Watch out for judgemental items which pose as success stories – for example, many celebrity magazines contain items about a celebrity's weight loss written in a way which is actually making a critical judgement about the person for having excess weight in the first place. Such items can reinforce negative views of your own starting point or journey and so have a demotivating effect. (A template is available at www. gettingyouthere.co.uk/life-in-the-driving-seat/resources).

Item	(1) Gossip	(2) Judgement /Blame	(3) Bad news	(4) Good news	(5) Success story	(6) Role model
Newspaper						
TV programme						
Book						
Radio show						
News show						

From now on, choose your reading and viewing materials so that you decrease the number of items that contain gossip, blame and bad news and increase those which contain good news, success stories and positive role models.

You aim isn't necessarily to start only reading and watching items which fit into those last three columns - just by being more aware of the nature of the material that you are immersing yourself in will help you choose a better balance for you. It can be helpful to set up a wish list of positive books, films and magazines that you would like to read, so there's always a selection to choose from when you have time to read or watch something.

❧❧❧❧❧❧❧

Feed your mind – and your imagination

After doing the activity above, you might be tempted to read only inspirational real-life stories and self-help books, ignoring fiction. This is not necessarily the best thing for you to do. As you discovered earlier in this book, your imagination is as important a factor in your success as your factual side is.

Just as you used the power of your imagination to understand what your vision for your future really is, it is your imagination that will help you come up with new and innovative ideas and solutions along the way. It is your imagination that enables you to imagine your success, develop your dreams and to relax. So don't forget to feed your imagination - read fiction alongside your factual books, watch films and visit the theatre, listen to radio dramas and to fiction on an audiobook. Engage your imagination on your journey and you will be amazed at the new ideas, concepts and solutions that it will help your mind create. These are also enjoyable activities which can make good rewards for milestones.

Peace and quiet

In today's world, it is often the case that we rarely spend time in peaceful quietness, simply allowing our minds to settle without planning, worrying, concentrating on a task or focusing on external dialogue from the television, radio or other people. However, it is times of quiet contemplation that we often have new ideas and inspirations. It also helps to reduce any sense of being overwhelmed on busy days.

In order to get the most out of your journey and to become aware of all of the opportunities around you, develop the habit of spending a least a few minutes a day without distraction. Whether you get up early enough to spend time before the day becomes hectic, or you make use of the time you walk the dog, the important thing is to let your mind think calmly without either worrying or working towards a specific purpose. Spending time each day in this way will increase your productivity and creativity, so it's well worth it.

A glance in the rear view mirror

In this chapter, you have:

- thought about how the things that you read, listen to and watch, affect how you see the world and your place in it.

- considered your mental inputs over the last few months and how you might benefit from changing them to more positive ones in the future.

- learned about the benefits of feeding your imagination through fiction, supporting your ability to be creative and innovative.

- planned to spend a few minutes of quiet time each day.

CHAPTER 7: STAYING ROADWORTHY

Throughout your journey, it is important that you take care to maintain your energy, enthusiasm and motivation. There will be times when the road seems tougher and your journey slows down. At other times, you might feel you are having to climb a steep slope.

In this chapter, we will look at how you can best take care of yourself during the journey so that you become resilient to the more stressful parts of it. You will learn some techniques for stress management, ways in which others can be of help and take a look at how routinely managing your stress levels and overall well-being will prevent breakdowns and unnecessary delays.

Routine servicing

In order to reach your destination in one piece and, having enjoyed the journey, you will need to take care of your health and well-being. Without an adequate supply of good fuel and energy along the way, you will soon find yourself parked up and unable to reach your destination.

When planning any new venture, it is not uncommon for people to focus first on the needs of others and then on the material resources they need. Quite often people ignore their own needs, or at best leave them until last. Yet, when you think about it logically, it becomes clear that it's not possible to help others or to make best use of your resources unless you have your own health and vitality.

Therefore, as you go along on your journey, it is essential that you perform regular maintenance and repair. To help you do this, here is a checklist of items to pay attention to, followed by some basic self-care guidance. If you make the maintenance of these things a priority on your journey, you should get to your destination feeling energised, motivated and happy. These are:

- Stress levels
- Sleep
- Nutrition

Let's have a look at each of these and how they can be managed in a way that keeps you healthy and enthusiastic throughout your journey.

Stress

The word *stress* has a number of connotations. Many think that stress is inherently a bad thing, something either to use as a reason for not doing anything challenging, or something to be denied at all costs.

The truth is that stress in itself is not necessarily a bad thing. Research has shown that a small degree of stress actually enhances our performance – improving memory and reaction times. In the right amount, it's what gives us a buzz. It is only when stress becomes prolonged and/or more intense that it becomes damaging. Then it has an adverse effect on us.

The damaging effects of chronic or intense stress can affect:

- **Physical health:** prolonged stress can impact upon your immune and inflammation systems and can affect your muscles too – resulting in stiffness and pain.

- **Sleep:** sleep is essential for memory formation, appetite control, creativity, problem-solving skills, and mood. Sleep is also the time when physical repair and renewal happens.

- **Mental health:** stress results in increased irritability and tearfulness. The lack of sleep resulting from stress also causes problems such as poor memory and loss of creativity.

- **Relationships:** our mood changes can damage relationships at home and at work.

- **Career or business:** the changes in mental function, mood and health can damage our careers and business.

Consequently, it is important to learn how to prevent your stress reaching the levels that can cause damage. A useful analogy is to imagine that your ability to handle stress is like a glass under a dripping tap. The drips of water are life's stresses and the glass is your capacity to handle stress. If you never take the opportunity to empty the glass, then the glass will fill up and eventually overflow. The drip that causes the overflow need not be any bigger than any other drip, it simply has to be one drip too many for the glass to hold.

This way of thinking about stress explains why sometimes it can seem to come out of the blue, triggered by the most trivial upset. What has happened is that the trivial event was just the final drip of stress that caused your stress glass to overflow. To prevent this happening to you, you need to find ways to release your stress regularly – to empty your stress glass. This will enable you to maximise your capacity to deal with stress as it occurs. To become more resilient to stress. The important thing is to discover your own ways to do this, finding ways which suit you and your lifestyle. Common examples are crafts, walking, reading, playing or listening to music or spending time with friends or family. In addition, guided relaxation, self-hypnosis, mindfulness and massage are powerful ways to manage stress (you can download a free relaxation MP3 from www.gettingyouthere.co.uk/life-in-the-driving-seat/resources).

One approach that can help you is to become aware of your own stressor, how much stress they cause you and what it is about them that causes you stress. Be aware that we each have our own stressors, which might be different from the stressors of the people around us. For example, some of us are stressed by the idea of speaking to an audience, but would happily take a flight to anywhere in the world. Others would be happy to speak to any audience, but quake at the thought of getting on a plane.

What causes these differences? How stressful we experience any event is determined by three key factors:

- Firstly, **our beliefs, past experiences and expectations** influence which things we are comfortable with, and which we find stressful. People often tend to be more stressed by the unfamiliar, with stress decreasing as an event becomes commonplace.

- Secondly, *our level of* stress depends upon **the level of control we believe ourselves to have** in the situation. If you feel that you have no choice in the things you do, that events happen to you rather than you being able to negotiate or contribute to them, then you will feel the effects of stress negatively. However, if you see that you have some control, some influence, over what is going on in your life, you will experience the events more positively. It comes down to whether you are a driver or a passenger in your life.

- Thirdly, **the circumstances of the event.** For example, you might have heard that moving house is one of the most stressful events in a person's life. Personally, I think this ignores the impact of circumstance. Of course, there could be considerable stress if you are moving house due to a family break-up, or you will be leaving behind friends and family due to your move. However, if you are moving house because you've won the lottery or you have found your dream job with a dream house, I doubt the stress will be the same. The circumstances make all the difference – they can add to the filling of your stress glass, or the emptying of it.

Next, you will look at some ways of becoming more resilient to stress. By increasing your resilience, you'll be able to get more enjoyment from your journey and to achieve more as you go.

Start with an empty glass

Do you ever find that you actually start your day feeling anxious or stressed – even before you've got out of bed? Do you already feel exhausted and feel the pressures of life bearing down on you by the time you start your day? When this happens, most people look to the quality of their sleep – assuming it's the quality or quantity of their sleep that needs improving in order to wake up feeling more refreshed and more resilient to stress.

This assumption is supported by the amount of advice on getting a good "sleep habit" - preparing for sleep by getting our evening habits arranged to increase our chances of a deep, refreshing sleep. Of course, good sleep is needed, but what if you have already got a good sleep habit and are still starting the day feeling stressed? Strangely there isn't much written about the importance of our "waking habit", yet the way we wake up sets us up for the day at least as much (if not more) than how we go to sleep.

For example, many of us wake to a fairly raucous alarm – a beeping, buzzing or ringing sound that jolts us awake. Well, that'll get the stress response going straight away. We then put the radio or television on. As we often wake up just as the news is coming on, stories of death, despair and arguing politicians fill our ears, eyes and minds. Our stress response increases. Then, to top it all off, we often have a couple doses of strong coffee just to get us going. Caffeine is known to stimulate adrenalin and so can further increase your stress response.

Sound familiar? So, maybe it's your waking habits that set you up for a stressful day, getting your stress response up and running before you've even left the house. If this sounds familiar to you, why not consider the alternatives:

- **Wake to pleasant music** – get an alarm clock which plays your music, or set your phone to play music instead of a ringtone

- **Delay listening to the news until later.** Continue with the music instead or listen to an audiobook if you're commuting

- **Decrease your morning caffeine intake.** Just have a single coffee (or even a decaff), or a different drink altogether.

Starting your day more gently lets you begin with a lower level of stress. You can't guarantee the rest of the day will be so calm, but at least you're starting off better.

Learn to say no

Do you often realise you've taken on more than you can really do? How often do you give up something you'd like to do for yourself because you've promised all of your time to other people? How often do you resent doing things for others?

If you find that you do one or more of these things, you could probably benefit from learning to say no. Don't blame others for always expecting you to do stuff for them – they're only reacting to how you've behaved in the past. We are each responsible for how we're perceived and, if you've always said yes in the past, you can hardly be surprised that folks expect you to say yes now.

If you do find that you are often in the situation described above, you could benefit from recognising and accepting the importance of your own needs and from managing other people's expectations of you. Start to set aside times for yourself and be willing to say no to other demands on that time. You can make it clear when you would be able to lend a hand, or do a job, but by making it clear that you value your time, others will learn to respect it too.

If you've been saying yes to people for a very long time it might take some getting used to, on both sides. Don't be bullied into sacrificing your own time for someone else's priorities – as adults, they are capable of finding alternatives and organising their own lives. This isn't about being mean or selfish – after all, you're not saying never.

What's more, by not taking on too much you'll be able to do the things you do take on more effectively. Remember, saying yes to everything leads people to believe your time has no value – after all, if you're willing to give it away, why should anyone think it valuable?

Laugh

Nothing reduces stress like laughing. Doesn't matter what causes it – silly kitten videos on YouTube, re-runs of old sitcoms, playing with your dogs or fooling around with the family – laughter is healthy and stress-busting.

Why not make it a habit for when you get home from work to find something which makes you laugh? Comedy shows playing while you prepare dinner perhaps, or watching short video clips while having a coffee break? When we laugh we see the world (including ourselves) more positively, which improves our ability to see opportunities and to feel good.

Avoiding getting stuck in the traffic

Feeling powerless is a major contributor to stress. Yet, so often, we get worked up about the things we have absolutely no influence over – new parking arrangements near work, the actions of complete strangers, even bad news that we hear from the other side of the world and which we cannot change. Trouble is, while we are getting angry or upset by these things, and spending time thinking and talking about them, we are wasting the time and energy we have to make our lives better for ourselves by changing those things we can affect.

For example, if we find out we have a health problem, we have a choice of whether to spend time asking "why me?" and bemoaning the unfairness of life (neither of which will change a single thing), or we could spend that time finding out and planning how to limit the impact of the condition – for example: what lifestyle and dietary changes could help? What is the best way to take the medication so that it has best chance of working? By focusing on those things which are under our control we can move forward and be less stressed.

Once again, the questions we ask ourselves when we hear such information are what make the difference between us feeling stressed or feeling fine. Therefore, whenever you find something taking up your thoughts and making you feel angry, worried or frustrated, ask yourself *"What can I do about this issue to change it?"* If there is something you can do – then do it by all means. However, if the honest answer is *"Nothing"*, then move on and use your time and energy for your own benefit.

Live your life as it happens, not in retrospect or in fear

How often do you think about the past and the future? Many people spend a lot of time mulling over past events feeling embarrassed, regretful, angry or looking back with rose-tinted spectacles. Others spend time worrying about the future, "what if? –ing" about worst-case scenarios. The fact is that neither the past nor the future exist.

The past has gone and is immutable and the future has yet to happen. The only time we can actually live our life is now, this instance. Unfortunately, we often miss the now because our heads are in the past or the future – what a waste of the time we actually have!

Worse – while we're thinking up the dreadful possibilities of a bad future, we're missing the opportunities we have to make for a great one.

Just think how different things could be, if you swapped every five minutes you spent worrying about the past or the future for five minutes spent on doing something positive now instead. Just try it – each time you find yourself thinking negatively, switch your focus onto what you're doing at the time - notice the sounds, the sights, and the interactions going on around you. This is real life happening in real time so this technique enables you to spend time in the present.

Asking for directions

When you have a plan of any sort it can be tempting to think that you have to do everything yourself to be regarded as a successful person. The truth is, however, that to be truly successful you will benefit from the support and advice of others who have either travelled this way before, or who have expertise that you lack. Just as when you go on any other road-trip, there are times when you need professional help to keep your vehicle roadworthy and to help you continue with your journey despite punctures and breakdowns.

A go-it-alone attitude is commonplace in those starting up in self-employment. Particularly at the start of their journey, as they take on every task in their business – the marketing, the accounts, the website, etc. They quickly become exhausted as they are not only building up the part of their business that is their passion and their skill – they are also doing a lot of things which they do not like or which they are not very good at. This approach is costly in terms of time and well-being and actually doesn't really help the business either.

This approach can be applied whatever your goal – whether a career/business goal or a personal one. You might get the time you need to work on your plan (including your stress management) by employing a per-hour based professional to do those home tasks that you don't enjoy, such as cleaning, ironing or administration. For many people, the time freed by doing this is worth far more than the cost, especially when you take the improvements in well-being and stress reduction into account.

Likewise, many embark upon an ambitious fitness goal without speaking to experts in training methods and nutrition, and then end up not getting the results they want. Some simply fall short of their goals; others over-train and under-eat resulting in injuries and illness to the extent that they never achieve the results they were aiming for.

As you travel your own personal journey to success and happiness, be honest with yourself about which areas you feel confident about and which you might benefit from expert advice. The next activity is a start to the process, and you can repeat the activity at intervals along your journey to ensure it stays up-to-date.

Activity

 In this activity, you are going to do an audit of your skills against the skills you need for your personal success and happiness.

An example table for you to do this process is shown below. Draw up a similar one listing the activities relevant to you in the first column:

Activity	Can I do it?	Do I want to do it?	Alternative
Financial planning	No	No	Outsource
Business planning	No	Yes	Find training course
Keep business premises clean and stocked	Yes	No	Outsource
Deliver training	Yes	Yes	-
Design fitness plan	No	No	Employ a personal trainer

(Template available from: www.gettingyouthere.co.uk/life-in-the-driving-seat/resources).

Once you have identified the things you can outsource and any skills you need to develop further, you can be even more confident that your journey to your vision will be exciting and successful.

The importance of breaks and down-time.

We've probably all been there – you see an actor in a film and just can't remember his or name, and realising you're missing the film while trying to think of it you just give up and get back to watching. Then later – hours, even days, afterwards - the answer pops into your head? Usually whilst doing a routine task such as having a shower or driving a familiar route.

It's a good example of how our subconscious mind carries on working away at a problem, even when we've stopped thinking consciously about the subject. It's as if, once asked a question, the processing part of the mind continues with it until it comes up with the answer. This is a really useful thing to be aware of. Often, when we have a problem to solve, we keep on thinking about it consciously. We might even think that if we take a break from thinking about it we're slacking off in some way, being lazy or giving up. Yet it's in the break from conscious thinking about a problem that the subconscious processing can occur – and the answer can be found.

There have been studies which show that, especially if a problem is complex, those who take a break before giving an answer come up with better answers than those who keep working away at it for the same length of time. Giving time for your subconscious to join all the information together is a really important part of the problem-solving process. The same is the case for coming up with creative ideas too.

Taking a break is important for many reasons – including managing stress levels, preventing mental fatigue, and for preventing muscle problems. Now you can take your breaks knowing that you're actually more likely to come up with that answer or idea you were wracking your brain for – and that can't be bad!

Be aware that, if you already suffer from stress, it might be that you have stopped doing many things that you enjoy – that is a common side effect of stress. Remind yourself of the activities, hobbies and social events that make you feel good – and schedule them in, as a recurring activity in your plan.

Relaxation and fun are not wasted time – you can't make the journey of a lifetime without looking after your vehicle and driver!

Sleep

Sleep is probably the most important resource for staying roadworthy throughout your journey. A tired brain gets stressed easily and is poor at problem-solving and thinking creatively. We all know that babies get cranky when tired, but we seem to forget that adults are no different. Tired people handle stress poorly and get emotional easily, and become angry, tearful, anxious and depressed easily too. It's not difficult to see how easily tiredness-related stress can become contagious as relationships are put to the test and those around us get stressed too.

Sleep is possibly one of the most under-estimated resources too. If you currently do not prioritise sleep, then now is a good time to change that. Stop seeing sleep as a luxury – sleep is as essential as air, water and food. In fact, if a person hasn't slept properly for a while, the need to sleep can overpower even the survival instinct – as happens when drivers fall asleep even whilst driving on a motorway.

All too often, people stay up late at night – watching television, reading, or chatting on Facebook. Perversely, we often stay up for hours later than we need to and yet would give anything for an extra hour in bed in the morning. If this sounds familiar, then set an alarm to go to bed half-hour earlier than usual and, if you feel reluctant, remember just how desirable that extra half-hour was when you awoke that morning.

The need for sleep is overwhelming and even mild to moderate sleep deprivation reduces a person's problem-solving abilities, creativity and memory, not to mention their tolerance and coping abilities. It can help if you think of yourself as if you were your phone – if you don't recharge your battery properly, you'll soon stop functioning until you do!

Nutrition: Filling the tank

Be aware that embarking on an exciting journey requires you to have the right fuel to keep you sustained and energetic. The better the fuel you choose, the better the results you will get in terms of well-being and resilience. Therefore, avoid any temptation to resort to fast food, processed meals and snacks, and excessive alcohol. Just as the concept of garbage-in/garbage-out applies to your mind, the same is true of your body.

Good nutrition need not be complicated. There are just five basic guidelines to follow:

- Whenever possible, choose foods which are natural or minimally processed

- Aim to avoid all foods and drinks which contain added sugars

- Have oily fish such as mackerel, sardines or salmon once or twice a week [1]

- Each day eat as many different colours of vegetables (including salads) as possible.

---

1) Be aware that the UK National Health service recommends "Women who are planning a pregnancy or who are currently pregnant or breastfeeding should eat no more than two portions of oily fish a week. This is because pollutants found in oily fish may affect the future development of a baby in the womb" source: http://www.nhs.uk/Livewell/Goodfood/Pages/fish-shellfish.aspx (14th July 2016)

- Aim to eat when hungry and stop when full, becoming aware of these two signals as much as possible.

Sticking to these simple guidelines, combined with staying hydrated, will keep you energised and provide you with what you need to make the most of your journey.

A glance in the rear view mirror

In this chapter, you have:

- discovered more about the importance of managing your stress levels.

- learned some techniques for becoming more resilient to stress.

- learned about the benefits of focusing on the things you can influence, and letting go of the things you can't.

- considered how delegation and advice from experts might speed up your progress and reduce your stress.

- discovered the importance of down-time for processing information and improving creativity and problem solving.

PART THREE: Your destination

"The feeling is less like an ending than just another starting point."

-Chuck Palahniuk,Choke

CHAPTER 8: ARRIVING AT YOUR DESTINATION

Congratulations! Your planning has paid off and you have now achieved your ambition – you have arrived at your destination and are ready to live the life you want.

If your journey has been a long and ambitious one, you might need to resist any temptation to immediately set off on your next one. Spend some time enjoying your success – and don't forget the reward you promised yourself for achieving it! Really allow yourself to appreciate your accomplishment and to recognise the work and determination that got you to the success you now have. Doing this will strengthen your motivation for your next journey.

Now that you've reached your destination, take time to become familiar with it – to get to know this new place. How closely does it match your vision? Is it what you wanted? If you identify there's still something else that you need to have the life you want, don't worry – you know now how to plan the journey to achieve that too. In terms of your overall life journey, it's simply a case of having arrived at the outskirts of your destination and following the directions to the exact spot.

Take time too to reflect upon what you've learned during your journey – to identify which things went well and which things you would change. Just as you reviewed your progress, you can now review your whole journey.

As you adjust to your success, notice how well you are managing your time now and be aware of whether or not you are stressed or tired. Remember your original reasons for wanting the achievement – have those reasons been satisfied? Has your journey invigorated you or exhausted you? Now that you have succeeded in those goals, you might want to start re-claiming some leisure time. This is where your next journey could take you. Just take a little time to adjust so that you become very familiar with your new situation.

You will probably find that your success will motivate you to choose another goal – to go on another journey. This time with even more confidence and excitement. Do allow time to appreciate your success first though. Then you can start thinking *"What next?"*

Planning your next journey

After being at your destination for a while, you might realise that you are ready to take another journey – maybe to upgrade your destination now that you realise how capable you are of achieving what you want for your future. It is possible that the effort of the journey, even though enjoyable, could have caused you to develop habits which you would now like to change. For example, goals which have included building a business or learning a new skill might have resulted in a habit of working or studying very long hours and you could decide that you can reduce those now.

You have gained so much experience and learned so many skills on your journey that you can feel confident that you can now plan the journey to your next goal, knowing that you have everything you need to succeed at that too.

Enjoy!

What next?

Are you ready to set out on an ambitious journey? Would like to work with Ann as your co-driver, providing motivation, support and guidance? Then why not get in touch to discover how engaging Ann as your coach could make your journey smoother and faster.

Ann can work face-to-face or via Skype to coach you to achieve your goals – however ambitious they are. If you would like to contact Ann, you can do so at ann@gettingyouthere.co.uk. You can also find out more about her work, and download other resources on her website at www.gettingyouthere.co.uk.

Whether you're looking for Life Coaching to achieve your dreams and ambitions and to have a more successful, more balanced lifestyle, Confidence Coaching to enable you to network and present your business effectively, or you want to improve your chances of promotion or career change with Career Coaching, invest now in one of these coaching programmes.

Start making your future a successful one right now! Feel free to get in touch with Ann to discuss your requirements.

WANT TO CHANGE WHERE YOU ARE IN LIFE, BUT NO IDEA WHAT YOU REALLY WANT INSTEAD?

Many people know what they want to move away from, but lack clarity about what they want to move to. That's why Ann developed The Coaching Conversation. This is a unique, transformational breakthrough coaching session designed to enable you to identify your direction and goals and begin planning your journey to achieve them.

The Coaching Conversation will kick-start your life's transformation into how you want it to be. Contact Ann for more details.

Coaching wherever you are!

Though Ann is based near **Hinckley** in Leicestershire, UK and provides face-to-face coaching, she can also provide coaching over the telephone or through Skype.

The Coaching Conversation

RESOURCES

I hope you have enjoyed this book and have used it as your guide to taking your personal journey to happiness and success.

All templates for the activities are available for download from my website at: www.gettingyouthere.co.uk/life-in-the-driving-seat/resources.

On the *Getting You There* website, you will also find a free relaxation MP3 download, which you can use to help you become more relaxed and confident. It provides 20 minutes of calmness and peace, so why not try it out?

Also on the *Getting You There* website you can register for the *Getting You There* newsletter to keep up-to-date with new resources and information to help you achieve.

www.gettingyouthere.co.uk.

STRESS MANAGEMENT APP

 Along with Steve, I have also produced an iPhone app (Hypnosis for happiness - Let go of anxiety) with a range of audio tracks to help you deal with a number of different stressors. Each track is available in either a female or a male voice, so you can pick the one you like best. The style and tone of narration will guide you peacefully to a place of tranquillity and security in which you can relax safely - both mentally and physically. In this state of calm relaxation it becomes easy to let go of your stress and to make those changes you want to make.

Hypnosis for happiness - Let go of anxiety includes some tracks to

- give you pure relaxation

- help you cope with stress

- weight management

- loneliness

- or even the need to control everything in your life.

We developed the app because we wanted more people to be able to experience the enjoyment and benefits of guided relaxation and self-hypnosis, and to discover for themselves how to make easy and beneficial changes in their lives through self-hypnosis. Over time, we will add new tracks to deal with other issues, along with more pure relaxation tracks. You can go to the app in ITunes by scanning in the QR code below:

ACKNOWLEDGEMENTS

There are a number of people without whom this book would never have been written and published.

The existence of this book owes much to my publisher, Sarah Houldcroft of Goldcrest Publishing, who showed me that it was possible for me to write my first book, and who kept me on track with her knowledge and experience.

The illustrations in this book were drawn and produced by Morgan Gleave of Morgan Gleave Art and Design. Morgan listened to what I wanted and was able to interpret my vague descriptions, turning them into exactly the illustrations I wanted.

I would also like to thank Louisa Sando-Patel for proofreading the final version and for spotting those times when my fingers had been uncoordinated and my editing less than thorough.

I'd especially like to thank my husband, Steve, for the support, patience and many cups of coffee provided generously throughout the time I was writing. He is the best co-driver I could possibly have in my life. The book could never have been completed without him.

A final thanks goes to Eddie and Juno, my two Parson terriers, who kept me company all the times I was at my desk writing, and who never let me forget the need for breaks and exercise!

ABOUT THE AUTHOR

Ann is an experienced and skilled coach and hypnotherapist. She works with clients to overcome their personal challenges and problems and to achieve their very best. Ann specialises in enabling people to build their confidence and self-belief and to achieve a level of self-understanding that makes achievement of their goals inevitable. After gaining her degree in Biological Sciences, Ann went on to Oxford University to train as a Science Teacher. As well as teaching, Ann also spent a number of years undertaking medical research. A change in personal circumstances caused her to leave research and to work closer to home where she developed her skills and knowledge of both the voluntary sector and the area of adult education, eventually moving to work on the implementation of national policy around post-16 education. Prior to training to be a therapist and coach, Ann was a senior manager in the public sector, directing the development and implementation of national programmes in the Further Education and Training sector. In that role, she gained a Master's degree in Education (Leadership and Management) and managed teams of diverse specialities, from mathematicians and statisticians to policy developers.

In 2007, Ann began training to become a hypnotherapist and a life coach. After gaining her Hypnotherapy Practitioner Diploma, Ann began training with one of the UK's foremost life coaches and coaching trainers, Curly Martin, and subsequently gained her Level 7 Diploma in Life Coaching. Ann is also an NLP Practitioner. Ann is an Accredited Coach with the International Institute of Coaching and Mentoring.

Ann now runs a busy coaching and therapy practice with her husband Steve in South-West Leicestershire. She manages her own stress through walking and playing with their two Parson terriers, Eddie and Juno, and through the pursuit of her hobby of photography. Ann and Steve's business, Getting You There, was established in 2008.

CONTACT ANN FINNEMORE

www.gettingyouthere.co.uk

success@gettingyouthere.co.uk

07523 198772

Twitter: @Ann_Finnemore

Facebook:
www.facebook.com/holistic.therapies.
in.Leicestershire/